TABLE OF CONTENTS

PREFACE

This book is designed to help you develop a meaningful and disciplined personal prayer life. I have heard people say, "I'd like to pray more, but after five minutes I run out of things to pray about." Most of us know what that's like. *Patterns for Prayer* is for all who have "run out of things to pray about."

Regular use of this prayer guide will help you

- learn to use the language of Scripture in prayer
- use all of the elements of prayer regularly
- claim the promises of God with confidence
- keep your thoughts from wandering during prayer
- pray expressively for friends and family
- release God's power and grace for your church and the kingdom of God
- develop the habit of praying for unsaved friends and acquaintances

You'll discover a weekly cycle in these pages as you pray for the leadership and ministries of your own local church. You'll pray about worship, church leaders, outreach ministries, church education, world missions, caregiving and fellowship, and financial stewardship.

This guide is meant to enlarge and deepen your prayer life. It is not intended to be the whole of it. Let these prayer suggestions trigger prayer expressions from your own heart. Where they do not fit, customize them to your own situation. Space is provided on each page for you to keep a record of further petitions and intercessions.

The Heidelberg Catechism reminds us that "God gives his grace and Holy Spirit only to those who pray continually and groan inwardly, asking God for these gifts and thanking him for them" (Q&A 116). I pray that you may do just that and, in so doing, find that your life is enriched as you grow in intimacy with God and receive a generous amount of his grace and Spirit.

—Alvin J. VanderGriend

MAY 1

Personal Prayer

Praise God for his holiness (Ex. 15:11). Thank him for calling you to live a life of holiness through the power of the Holy Spirit. Confess contentment with areas of your life that do not reflect God's holiness. Commit yourself to avoiding anything that "contaminates body and spirit" (2 Cor. 7:1). Ask God to give you a daily desire to obey his command to "be holy, because I am holy" (Lev. 11:45).

For Your Family and Friends

Pray for the teens in your family or among your friends. Ask God to protect them from all the "contaminants" offered by our modern culture.

For the Church

Thank God for the leaders in your congregation. Ask that they would be committed to personal holiness. Pray also for their marriages and families.

For the Kingdom

Pray that God would be glorified throughout his kingdom as it spreads around the world. Ask for renewal to sweep the churches of the West. Thank God for great harvests in the former Soviet Union, in Asia, and in South America.

For the Unsaved

Ask God to open the eyes and hearts of unsaved friends. Pray for an opportunity this week to share the good news with at least one other person.

Patterns *for* Prayer

Volume 2: May - August

Alvin VanderGriend

Love2Pray

PrayerShop Publishing

Terre Haute, Indiana

PrayerShop Publishing is the publishing arm of the Church Prayer Leaders Network. The Church Prayer Leaders Network exists to equip and inspire local churches and their prayer leaders in their desire to disciple their people in prayer and to become a "house of prayer for all nations." Its online store, prayershop.org, has more than 150 prayer resources available for purchase or download.

ISBN (Print): 978-1-970176-15-5

ISBN (E-Book): 978-1-970176-16-2

Original contributors to this prayer guide include Edith Bajema, Dian Ginter, Joan Huyser-Honig, Don McCrory, Laurie Quist, Al Schaap, Mark Timmer, Alvin J. VanderGriend, and Jean Westenbroek.

MAY 2

Personal Prayer

Praise God for communicating with you in his inspired Word. Thank him for providing a "lamp to [your] feet and a light to [your] path" (Ps. 119:105). Confess any doubts you've harbored concerning the authority of God's Word in your life. Commit yourself to treasuring the words of God more than daily bread (Job 23:12). Ask God to feed you spiritually as you look to his Word for guidance throughout this week.

For Your Family and Friends

Think of one specific family. Pray that this family would set aside time every day for family devotions and prayer. Ask God to make this practice a blessing in their family life.

For the Church

Thank God for the outreach ministries of your congregation. Pray for the work of your deacons. Pray for the ministries of mercy which they perform on your behalf.

For the Kingdom

Pray for Bible publishers and distribution agencies, such as the Gideons, who make the Word of God readily available to millions of people. Ask that God will prosper their work and witness.

For the Unsaved

Ask that unsaved people you know will discover the irresistible sweetness of God's Word (Ps. 119:103) and be drawn to Christ through it.

Prayer Pointer

"The answer of our prayers is secured by the fact that in rejecting them God would in a certain sense deny his own nature."—John Calvin

MAY 3

Personal Prayer

God sends his teaching like rain and his words like the dew (Deut. 32:2). Praise God for being your teacher (Ps. 71:17). Thank God for the privilege of receiving his instruction through his Word. Confess any lack of attention you've paid to God's teaching. Commit yourself to listening closely to what God has to say to you. Ask God to reveal himself more clearly through his Word each day.

For Your Family and Friends

Pray for the parents in Christian families close to you. Ask God to help them to be excellent teachers and role models for their children.

For the Church

Pray for the teachers and helpers in your church school program. Thank God for their dedication and hard work. Pray also for adult education classes and teachers.

For the Kingdom

Thank God for the work of Christians who are helping to refocus the educational system in the former Soviet Union. Pray for Russian teachers who now have much greater freedom to present biblical truths in the classroom.

For the Unsaved

Ask that God will shower the blessings of salvation on unsaved people in your community as they learn of Christ.

MAY 4

Personal Prayer

Praise God, whose name is great among the nations (Mal. 1:11). Give thanks that the gospel has reached around the world and into your heart. Confess any sin that has hindered you from gaining a clear vision of God's work in the world. Commit yourself to God's plan for the gospel to be preached in the whole world (Mt. 24:14). Ask God to use you in that plan.

For Your Family and Friends

Pray for the children and teens among your family and friends. Ask that the gospel of the kingdom will take root among them at an early age.

For the Church

Boldly intercede for the work of gospel missions worldwide. Pray by name for world missionaries whom your church supports. Ask God to protect them and prosper their work.

For the Kingdom

Thank God that one day "all the ends of the earth will remember and turn to the LORD, and all the families of the nations will bow down before him" (Ps. 22:27). Ask that that special day will arrive soon.

For the Unsaved

Ask God to burden your heart with the plight of one unsaved person you know. Pray for that person by name. Ask that God's global mission will touch that one soul and spark new life in Christ.

MAY 5

Personal Prayer

Praise God for his great love and mercy shown to you (Eph 2:4). Give thanks that nothing can separate you from the love of Jesus (Rom. 8:35). Confess any lack of love which you have shown to God or to another person. Commit yourself to loving God with your whole being (Deut. 6:5). Ask God to prune your life so that the spiritual fruit of love will grow large and appetizing to others.

For Your Family and Friends

Ask God to root out all hatred, jealousies, anger, and bitterness that may have sprouted up in your family life. Pray for love to grow in every relationship.

For the Church

How do the members of your church show love to one another and to their neighbors? Pray for fellowship and caregiving programs in your congregation.

For the Kingdom

Ask God to bring an end to civil wars, urban violence, racial bigotry, economic injustice, and every other sin that scars nations and neighborhoods. Pray for love to reign instead of hate.

For the Unsaved

It was Jesus' love for sinners that sent him to the cross. Pray for an opportunity to share that kind of sacrificial love with another person (Jn. 15:9).

Prayer Pointer

"Beyond the preoccupation we all have with our needs, the rock-bottom reality of prayer is the sharing of experience." —Michael Card

MAY 6

Personal Prayer

Praise God, who is the source of all wealth and prosperity on earth (1 Chron. 29:12). Give thanks for all the material blessings God has given to you. Confess any occasions when you have tried to "store up for yourself treasures on earth" (Mt. 6:19). Commit yourself to remembering that wealth and possessions, and the ability to enjoy them, are a gift from God (Eccl. 5:19). Ask him to open your eyes to new opportunities to use your possessions for the benefit of others.

For Your Family and Friends

Pray for family members or friends who have difficulty managing their household finances. Ask God to provide the help they need to be better managers.

For the Church

Pray for the deacons of your church. Thank God for their integrity and honesty as they handle the financial resources of your congregation. Pray also that your congregation will be a church of cheerful givers.

For the Kingdom

Ask God to raise up people to contribute generously to the ministries of the church worldwide. Pray that real needs will be met without undue strain. Pray also that contributions will be used wisely.

For the Unsaved

Pray Eph. 1:18 for any unsaved person you know, asking especially that his or her spiritual eyes will be opened to see the eternal treasure of life in Christ.

MAY 7

Personal Prayer

Glorify God as the beginning and end of all things, the Alpha and the Omega. Give thanks for his love for you—a love that has kept you in mind since the beginning of the world and will continue to hold you when this world has passed away. Confess those times when you have seen yourself and your needs as the beginning and end of your existence. Commit yourself to giving God the highest place in your life and heart. Ask God to reveal his glory to you so that you cannot help but praise him with your whole heart.

For Your Family and Friends

Pray for the children in your family and congregation, that they may receive a blessing and a sense of God's love and presence in worship.

For the Church

Pray for worship leaders in your congregation, that they may see the Alpha and the Omega, the Living One whose "face was like the sun shining in all its brilliance" (Rev. 1:16-18) and lead the people in praise of the Lord.

For the Kingdom

Pray that worship services all over the world will glorify the name and power of Jesus rather than promote lesser things.

For the Unsaved

Ask God to reveal his glory and power to any unbelievers who attend worship services in your community, so that they begin to worship him.

MAY 8

Personal Prayer

Praise your Father as the God of gods and the Lord of kings and a revealer of mysteries (Dan. 2:47). Give thanks for the mystery of salvation through Christ, which has been revealed to you through God's Word and Spirit (Eph. 3:3-6). Confess that there are times when you do not rely on his wisdom and insight in your daily struggles. Commit yourself to spending more time in God's Word and prayer, seeking to understand the mystery of your life in Christ. Ask God to fill you with a spirit of wisdom and revelation (Eph. 1:17).

For Your Family and Friends

Pray for those you know whose minds have been blinded by the gods of this age, unable to see the light of the gospel of the glory of Christ (2 Cor. 4:4).

For the Church

Ask God that the leaders in your congregation may be especially gifted with wisdom as they lead your members through the challenges that you face in your neighborhood, outreach, and nurturing programs.

For the Kingdom

Pray especially for Christian leaders in strife-torn areas, that they may have the wisdom to speak God's Word in difficult situations and bring truth and love where there is hatred and division.

For the Unsaved

Pray for one family on your street who does not attend church. Ask God to give you the opportunity to speak to them within the next few weeks.

MAY 9

Personal Prayer

Praise God as a rock of refuge, as a shelter, as a safe dwelling place (Ps. 31:3, 20). Give thanks that you have been rescued from forces in this world that would have overwhelmed your soul. Confess those times when you have paid little attention to the safety and refuge he offers. Commit yourself to remaining under the shadow of his protection. Ask God to shelter you this day.

For Your Family and Friends

Ask God to be a shelter and protection to single-parent families. Pray that the children of divorced parents will especially feel God's loving presence.

For the Church

Pray that your congregation may offer the security of God, our rock, to those in your neighborhood who live in fear of death, poverty, crime, sickness, or loneliness.

For the Kingdom

Pray that God will be especially close to those Christians around the world who are imprisoned or persecuted for their faith. Ask that they may sense your prayers around them like a shelter and a cloak of protection.

For the Unsaved

Pray for those in nursing homes who are dying without the assurance of God's love to welcome them home. Ask God to send people to tell them about Jesus, the rock of our salvation.

Prayer Pointer

"The first stage of prayer is not an activity of mind but a passive mode of receiving. Like slipping into a tub of hot water, I let God's love seep in, saturate, permeate every part of my being." —Brennan Manning

MAY 10

Personal Prayer

Give praise to the one who said, "I am . . . the truth" (Jn. 14:6). Thank God for rescuing you from the darkness of Satan's deceit and placing you in the kingdom of his marvelous light (1 Pet. 2:9). Repent of those times that you have been uncomfortable with the light of God's truth and have preferred twisting the truth to suit your purposes. Commit yourself to walking in the light of God's truth with your whole heart. Ask God to make you willing to do that, no matter the cost to your pride or reputation.

For Your Family and Friends

Ask God to build truthful relationships between parents and children. Pray that God will restore trust and love so that children can be honest about their feelings and problems.

For the Church

Pray that your church's education classes will help those who struggle with Satan's deceit in their lives to come to know the truth in Christ.

For the Kingdom

Pray that those in government, especially judges and lawmakers, will make their decisions in the light of God's truth. Ask that they not be influenced by Satan's claim that there is no God and no standard of truth.

For the Unsaved

Ask God to use your example of honesty and truthfulness this week to move someone's heart to see the reality of God.

MAY 11

Personal Prayer

Praise the Lamb of God, who was beaten and crucified for the sins of the world. Thank him for taking your place, your punishment, your sins on himself. Confess the sins that have been on your conscience this past week, knowing that God will deal gently with you (Heb. 4:14-16). Commit yourself to living for Christ, not for the empty way of life that his blood redeemed you from (1 Pet. 1:18-19). Ask Jesus to help you understand the depth of the love that sent him to the cross for you.

For Your Family and Friends

Pray that the Christian singles you know may be kept free from immorality and may give their full energy and time to the Lord's work (1 Cor. 7:32-35).

For the Church

Pray for the children and young people in your congregation that God is already preparing to become missionaries. Ask God to use you to encourage them and to set an example for them by your interest and support of world missions.

For the Kingdom

Intercede for specific missionaries that you know, asking God to protect them from evil, provide for all their financial needs, and encourage them by giving a good response to their message.

For the Unsaved

Pray especially for the millions of Muslims around the world, that God will break through their darkness and help them find freedom and forgiveness in Christ's blood.

MAY 12

Personal Prayer

Praise the Father who has compassion on his children. Thank him for forgiving all your sins, healing all your diseases, redeeming your life from the pit, crowning you with love and compassion, and satisfying your desires with good things (Psalm 103). Confess those periods in your day when you are unaware of God's faithful, watching, loving presence beside you and within you. Commit yourself to watching for signs of his love and tenderness toward you. Ask him to draw you closer to himself.

For Your Friends and Family

Pray for families where you suspect abuse, that God will provide healing, protection, and love for those who suffer.

For the Church

Pray that the oil of God's love will be like a sweet scent in all the activities of your church's fellowship this week. Ask God to let you share his love in a specific way with at least one other church member this week.

For the Kingdom

Pray for "those who are least in the kingdom of heaven"—the poor, sick, lonely, outcast, struggling, grieving—that they may find the Father's love in a warm church fellowship.

For the Unsaved

Pray that through your loving concern this week, one person may be brought closer to the kingdom of God.

MAY 13

Personal Prayer

Praise the Creator of the stars, the sun, the sky, the earth, and all life in this vast creation. Thank him for having created you and providing for all your needs. Confess the doubts you've had that God could supply your needs from the storehouse of his abundance. Commit yourself to a way of giving that is as generous and loving as your Father's. Ask God to continue to supply all your needs.

For Your Family and Friends

Ask God to meet the needs of families who struggle to make ends meet financially. Pray that their eyes will be turned to the Lord and to his ability to provide.

For the Church

Pray that believers will be moved to honor God by bringing him the full tithes from their earnings. Ask that they will depend on God to "throw open the floodgates of heaven and pour out so much blessing that [they] will not have room enough for it" (Mal. 3:10).

For the Kingdom

Ask God to help all believers make him Lord of their finances as well as every other area of life. Pray for wisdom in financial dealings, in spending, in investing, and in giving for all Christians.

For the Unsaved

Pray that as people receive financial and material assistance from churches, they will see God's love for them and turn to him for salvation.

MAY 14

Personal Prayer

Praise the Lamb, Jesus Christ, who with his blood "purchased men for God from every tribe and language and people and nation" (Rev. 5:9). Thank the Lord that he covenanted with Abraham long ago and that you have the blessing of being part of God's own people. Confess any tendencies that you have to judge people by color, ethnicity, or background. Commit yourself to showing no favoritism, just as God shows none (Acts 10:34). Ask that you will do your part in the kingdom of priests who serve God (Rev. 5:10).

For Your Family and Friends

Give thanks for the gifts, abilities, and perspectives of those whom God has given to you, and ask his blessing upon them.

For the Church

Pray that the worshipers of your own church body will have a sense of the church as it gathers in many places throughout your community and the world. Pray that you and your fellow believers will not be cliquish or divisive.

For the Kingdom

Ask that the power of racism in our society will be broken, and that Christians will lead the way in this.

For the Unsaved

Pray that specific non-Christians around you will understand that God looks upon the heart, and that they will seek to have their hearts made right through Christ.

MAY 15

Personal Prayer

Praise the Lord God Almighty, whose deeds are great and marvelous. Thank God for the opportunity to become godly, and that "godliness has value for all things, holding promise for both the present life and the life to come" (1 Tim. 4:8). Confess your lack of the devotion to God which results in a life pleasing to him. Commit yourself to a life of compassion, kindness, humility, gentleness and patience (Col. 3:12). Ask that the grace of God will teach you "to say 'No' to ungodliness and worldly passions, and to live [a] self-controlled, upright and godly [life] in this present age" (Titus 2:12).

For Your Family and Friends

Pray that your family and friends will make godliness a priority, and that your own godliness will be a real encouragement to them.

For the Church

Pray that your church leaders will be uncompromising examples of godliness for your congregation. Ask that they will receive consistent support from the congregation.

For the Kingdom

Pray for "kings and all those in authority, that we may live peaceful and quiet lives in all godliness and holiness" (1 Tim. 2:2).

For the Unsaved

Pray that Jesus will become the Lord of the non-Christians around you.

MAY 16

Personal Prayer

Praise the Lord, your Savior and your God. Thank God for the hope that he gives to you and for the fact that he never forgets you. Confess all the desires which you have that crowd out your desire for God himself. Commit your soul to panting after God "as the deer pants for streams of water" (Ps. 42:1). Ask that you will "delight yourself in the LORD and [that he will give] you the desires of your heart" (Ps. 37:4).

For Your Family and Friends

Ask God to cause your friends and family to have a deep thirst for him, and to allow nothing else to quench that thirst.

For the Church

Pray that your church's efforts to reach others for Christ will be driven by a deep desire for people to experience what you have experienced in Christ.

For the Kingdom

Pray that your local and regional government leaders will come to know Christ and give him glory by making decisions according to his will. Pray for strength for Christians in government.

For the Unsaved

Jesus said, "Whoever drinks the water I give him will never thirst" (Jn. 4:14). Pray that three unsaved persons you know will drink the living water from Jesus.

Prayer Pointer

"Do not work so hard for Christ that you have no strength to pray, for prayer requires strength."—J. HUDSON TAYLOR

MAY 17

Personal Prayer

Praise God as the master even of the grave. Thank the Father that "Christ has indeed been raised from the dead, the firstfruits of those who have fallen asleep" (1 Cor. 15:20). Confess your failure to place your life and death fully in the hands of the risen Christ. Commit yourself to standing firm in the victory which Christ has achieved over sin and death and hell. Ask that you will "know that your labor in the Lord is not in vain" (15:58), and so work with extra fervor.

For Your Family and Friends

Pray that your family and friends will be energetic in their living for Christ. Give special thanks for those who already do this.

For the Church

Pray that the people of your congregation will become well-grounded in the basics of the Scriptures, and that they will faithfully live their beliefs.

For the Kingdom

Give thanks for your local law enforcement, fire protection, and emergency personnel, and ask God's blessing on their work.

For the Unsaved

Ask that several non-Christians (name them) will come to believe, and so, at the return of Christ, "bear the likeness of the man from heaven" (15:49).

MAY 18

Personal Prayer

Praise God as your faithful Creator and Re-creator in Christ. Give thanks that you can "participate in the sufferings of Christ, so that you may be overjoyed when his glory is revealed" (1 Pet. 4:13). Confess the times in which you have shirked responsibility by failing to speak or act for Christ. Commit yourself to living up to the weighty name "Christian." Ask that you will never "repay evil with evil or insult with insult" (1 Pet. 3:9).

For Your Family and Friends

Ask that your family and friends will not be ashamed of their faith, but will openly share what God has done for them.

For the Church

Thank the Lord for missionaries, and pray that he will be glorified by people being won for Christ through their work. Ask for patience for those workers.

For the Kingdom

Pray for people who are experiencing the effects of natural disasters. Pray that they will feel the closeness of God even in the turmoil, and that relief will be offered to them in Jesus' name.

For the Unsaved

Pray that unsaved persons whom you know will hear of and understand God's judgment and love, and respond by trusting in Christ alone.

Prayer Pointer

"I have to hurry all day to get time to pray." —MARTIN LUTHER

MAY 19

Personal Prayer

Praise the Lord, "the compassionate and gracious God, slow to anger, abounding in love and faithfulness" (Ex. 34:6). Thank God that you have been forgiven of all your sins because of Jesus' work for you. Confess in detail your sins, asking for a greater awareness of sin in your life. Commit yourself to putting on "the new self, created to be like God in true righteousness and holiness" (Eph. 4:24). Ask "to be made new in the attitude of your [mind]" (Eph. 4:23).

For Your Family and Friends

Pray that all your family and friends will daily seek God's gracious forgiveness and will live fitting Christian lives.

For the Church

Pray that no animosities or rivalries will be at home in your congregation, and that your congregation will experience peace and wholeness. Ask that you and your fellow Christians will prize the healthy relationships which you have with each other.

For the Kingdom

Pray for your local educational systems—staff, administration, board, students, and parents. Ask that they will honor God by what they do. Pray that anything which does not meet with God's approval will be rooted out.

For the Unsaved

Ask that acquaintances who do not know Jesus will become conscious of sin and seek his forgiveness.

MAY 20

Personal Prayer

Praise God as the constant and loving provider for all your needs. Give thanks to the Lord that his grace is sufficient for you (2 Cor. 12:9). Confess any times you have questioned the Lord's dealing with you and others. Commit yourself to "be content whatever the circumstances" (Phil. 4:11). Ask that daily you may confidently say, "I can do everything through him who gives me strength" (Phil. 4:13).

For Your Family and Friends

Pray that your friends and family members will base their attitudes and actions on their status in Christ and not their status in the world.

For the Church

Ask that contentment and dependence upon God will be expressed in your congregation's giving. Pray that Christians will understand giving as a prime part of their worship life.

For the Kingdom

Pray that Christians will not relinquish their ministry to governmental agencies and programs. Ask that Christians will work together to meet needs locally and worldwide and thereby be a visible expression of the power of Jesus Christ.

For the Unsaved

Pray that specific "Christ-less" individuals whom you know will be discontented with life without Christ, and seek life in him. Ask for the privilege of being involved in their conversion.

MAY 21

Personal Prayer

Praise God as the one from whom all things have come; praise him as the one to whom you are going when you are called home. Thank God that your relationship with him extends beyond this life. Confess the times when your focus has been only on physical needs, not God's eternal purpose for you (Mt. 6:33). Commit yourself to seeking God's will for you and to hearing the voice of his Spirit through the preaching of the Word. Ask God to reveal himself to you in his splendor and glory.

For Your Family and Friends

Pray that as your family members and friends worship, God may "give [them] the Spirit of wisdom and revelation, so that [they] may know him better" (Eph. 1:17).

For the Church

Pray that people in your congregation may worship with more of a desire to praise the living God than to be pleased or entertained.

For the Kingdom

Pray for those preachers in other countries who must serve eight or ten churches at a time. Ask God to give them strength and to provide lay leaders who can minister in their absence.

For the Unsaved

Ask God to put in the hearts of unsaved friends a hunger for him and for the warmth of fellowship in a local church.

MAY 22

Personal Prayer

Praise God as the great and powerful Creator who has no equal on earth or in the spiritual realm. Give thanks for the vast, eternal reaches of God's knowledge and wisdom. Confess those times when you have not trusted in God's leading. Commit yourself to spending more of your prayer time meditating on the depth of his knowledge and understanding. Ask God to daily make you aware of his power, his wisdom, and his great love for you.

For Your Family and Friends

Pray that the families in your congregation will make a special point of seeking God's will together daily in prayer.

For the Church

Pray that your pastor and elders will spend increasingly more time in prayer for God's guidance in the direction of the church, relying on the Spirit's leading and the instruction of God's Word (Acts 6:4).

For the Kingdom

Pray that those who have been called by God to intercede for Christian leaders and ministers will be faithful in this vital means of supporting the kingdom of God and its leaders (2 Thess. 3:1).

For the Unsaved

Pray for unsaved people you know who are struggling to find direction and meaning for their lives. Ask God to use you to speak to them with a wisdom they cannot resist (1 Cor. 1:23-25).

MAY 23

Personal Prayer

Praise God as the provider and sustainer of all things (Ps. 145:15-16). Give thanks for the tenderness and the care that the Lord gives to the creatures that he has made (145:8-9). Confess those times this past week when you have forgotten to look on other people or other parts of God's world with the same love that is in God's heart. Commit yourself to treating others with the same compassion as God does. Ask God to fill your heart with his care, concern, and tenderness.

For Your Family and Friends

Pray for families in which the parents are too busy to really listen and respond to their children's needs. Ask God to help them set their priorities in line with his will for their families.

For the Church

Pray for the deacons who work in your area or community, asking God's Spirit to charge their work with energy, compassion, and love for those who come seeking their help.

For the Kingdom

Pray for specific missionaries that your church supports, that God will enable them to identify more closely with the people and cultures they serve. Pray for understanding and encouragement in the face of cultural differences.

For the Unsaved

Pray for those you know who are not only outside of the family of God but also outside of your own cultural "family." Ask for an opportunity to talk with such a person this week, sharing God's love and concern for him or her.

MAY 24

Personal Prayer

Praise God as the Rock, your stronghold and fortress (Ps. 144:1-2). Thank him for being a solid foundation on which to stand spiritually, so that nothing can shake you (Mt. 7:24-25). Confess those times in your life when you have stepped off the rock solid foundation of God's Word and relied on your own understanding. Commit yourself to building your life on Christ's teachings. Ask God to help you plant your feet firmly in his Word each day.

For Your Family and Friends

Pray for the devotional times of the families that you know, that regular times of prayer and Bible reading will help bond family members to each other and to God. Pray that your single friends may find a group of spiritual brothers and sisters to do this with as well.

For the Church

Pray for those who teach adult and children's education classes in your church, that they may find the time for new learning themselves, for new growth in their spiritual lives.

For the Kingdom

Pray for those who write educational books and materials for the Church, that they may be moved by God's Spirit to touch on the needs of their readers and to write clearly the truths of Scripture.

For the Unsaved

Ask God to bring your unsaved friends into a knowledge of the truth, so that they can rest their feet on the solid rock of Christ's offer of complete salvation for them.

MAY 25

Personal Prayer

Give praise to God as the Comforter, who feels deeply for those who have been mistreated and abandoned (Isa. 49:13). Thank him for calling many believers into compassionate ministries for the sake of those who are suffering. Confess those times when you may have withheld comfort from others who needed it. Commit yourself to receiving God's encouragement and grace each morning and allowing that to flow through you to others. Ask God to fill you with the knowledge of his love, so that you may be filled with all the fullness of God (Eph. 3:19).

For Your Family and Friends

Pray that families in your church will open their homes to others who do not have a loving family to turn to.

For the Church

Pray for those in your church's neighborhood who have no family or friends to turn to. Ask that God will touch their lives through your calls, visits, and expressions of concern.

For the Kingdom

Pray for the efforts of disaster relief teams from churches all over the world. Ask God to make their compassion and commitment a shining light to people who have been struck by famine, storm, earthquake, or poverty.

For the Unsaved

Ask God to show himself to the unsaved who live on your street as a God who saves, as one who daily bears our burdens (Ps. 68:19-20).

MAY 26

Personal Prayer

Praise God as the eternal and triune God—the mystery of God in three persons of Father, Son, and Holy Spirit. Thank him for promising to make all believers one, just as the three persons of God are one (Jn. 17:20-23). Confess any tendency in your conversations or thoughts to work against this oneness of mind and purpose in the church. Commit yourself to working toward the unity of believers that is beautiful in God's sight (Psalm 133). Ask God to make you more sensitive to his will and purpose in this area.

For Your Family and Friends

Pray for those who are experiencing alienation from their families for the sake of their faith in God and their desire to follow Jesus (Lk. 12:52-53).

For the Church

Pray that less important issues and controversies not be allowed to prevent the church from "being like-minded, having the same love, being one in spirit and purpose" (Phil. 2:2).

For the Kingdom

Pray that Satan not be able to break the unity and fellowship of missionaries from different denominations and cultural backgrounds as they minister together in their common fields.

For the Unsaved

Pray that many outside the church will be convicted of the truth of the gospel when they see the unity and love that prevails in your church fellowship (Jn. 17:23).

MAY 27

Personal Prayer

Glorify the Son of God as one who is worthy to receive all power, wealth, wisdom, strength, honor, glory, and praise (Rev. 5:12). Thank him for having given up all this to die on a cross in your place. Confess any times when you have put your own interests above those of God and others. Commit yourself to being a faithful disciple of Jesus, finding your life by losing it for him and the gospel (Mk. 8:35). Ask Jesus to help you understand what it means to deny yourself, take up your cross, and follow him.

For Your Family and Friends

Pray that family and friends will be kept from a materialistic lifestyle that serves money rather than God (Lk. 16:13).

For the Church

Pray that believers will consider God's priorities as they set their budgets and plan their giving this week.

For the Kingdom

Pray that the money collected from tithes and offerings around the world will be used for the very best purposes, according to God's plan (2 Cor. 9:12).

For the Unsaved

Ask God to show your unsaved friends the emptiness of their pursuit for possessions and security (Lk. 12:15).

Prayer Pointer

"The greater our empathy and the more closely we identify through compassion with those for whom we pray, the more perfect is our communion with the merciful God." —Anthony Bloom

MAY 28

Personal Prayer

Praise your Father in heaven (Mt. 6:9). Thank him for including you as a son or daughter in his family. Confess moments when you've acted like an orphan, turning your back on God's fatherly love. Commit yourself to deeper fellowship with your Father. Ask him to reveal his abiding love in your life through his Word and Spirit.

For Your Family and Friends

Intercede for children in your family or community who are growing up without a mom or dad in the home. Pray for single parents whom you know.

For the Church

As you gather for worship with your brothers and sisters, ask the Father to quell any jealousies or sibling rivalries that would mar your church's worship and fellowship (Eph. 4:2).

For the Kingdom

Pray for war-torn areas of the world where parents and children are suffering deprivation, separation, and death. Ask the Father to bring peace on earth.

For the Unsaved

Think of one friend or coworker who has not experienced God's fatherly love in a redeeming way. Pray for an opportunity this week to speak to that person of the hope that you have (Eph. 2:12; 1 Pet. 3:15).

Prayer Pointer

"God's chief gift to those who seek him is himself." —E. B. Pusey

MAY 29

Personal Prayer

Praise the name of God (Mt. 6:9). Thank God for revealing his name to you through his Word and Spirit (Ex. 3:15). Confess times when you have misused the name of God in word or deed. Commit yourself to living in a way which hallows God's name. Ask God to glorify his majestic name in all the earth (Ps. 8:1).

For Your Family and Friends

If you have believing relatives and friends, thank God for calling them by his name into his family. Pray for their spiritual well-being. Intercede also for those who do not yet know Jesus.

For the Church

Pray for the pastor, elders, deacons, and other leaders in your congregation. Ask that their walk with the Lord will be vibrant and alive.

For the Kingdom

Pray for Christians working in public service. Ask that they will have the courage to hallow the name of God without compromise in their daily work.

For the Unsaved

Ask God to bless the work of missionaries who preach the gospel in unfamiliar surroundings. Pray that they will be encouraged by Joel's prophecy that "everyone who calls on the name of the LORD will be saved" (Joel 2:32).

MAY 30

Personal Prayer

Praise King Jesus, who today rules and reigns over his kingdom (Mt. 6:10). Thank him for including you as a citizen of his earthly and heavenly realm. Confess any disloyalty you've felt as one of Christ's much-beloved subjects. Commit yourself to serving as an agent of peace in God's kingdom. Ask that all of Satan's attempts to overthrow this divine government will come to nothing.

For Your Family and Friends

Pray that God will protect your family from the realities of the kingdom of darkness and the power of Satan.

For the Church

Ask God to prosper the outreach ministries of your congregation. Pray that the lost and hurting in your community may be found and brought to Christ.

For the Kingdom

Thank God that his kingdom has no end (Dan. 7:27) and that it extends to every corner of the map (Ps. 103:19). Pray for revival in countries where the church is weak and has lost its way.

For the Unsaved

Pray that those who are not yet citizens of the kingdom of heaven will be drawn by the irresistible power of the Holy Spirit. Ask that you might be used to bring them in.

Prayer Pointer

"Prayer is the most difficult and costly activity of the Christian." —Alan Walker

MAY 31

Personal Prayer

Praise your Father for his perfect will (Mt. 6:10). Give thanks that nothing occurs in life that God does not cause to happen. Confess those times when you've doubted that his will was best for you. Commit yourself to living by Ps. 40:8: "I desire to do your will, O my God." Ask that God's perfect will may be accomplished in your life.

For Your Family and Friends

Intercede for teens in your family who face strong temptations from many sides. Ask God to protect them from making unwise decisions (1 Thess. 4:3-5).

For the Church

Ask God to bless the work of your Sunday school teachers and assistants. Pray also for the children and adults who attend your church's educational programs. Pray that the hearts of the children and youth will be turned toward God.

For the Kingdom

Take a global perspective. Pray for God's will to be done on earth even as it is in heaven. Ask that Satan's dark dominion will be exposed by the pure light of the gospel.

For the Unsaved

Ask God to make his will known to unsaved persons whom you know. Pray that they might find freedom from the bondage of sin. Ask God to show you how you can help them find Christ.

JUNE 1

Personal Prayer

Praise the God who supplies all your needs. Give thanks for the many material blessings you enjoy in this life. Confess any dissatisfaction or jealousy you have felt about God's provision for you. Commit yourself to living a truly thankful life. Ask God to give you today your daily bread (Mt. 6:11).

For Your Family and Friends

Pray for those who lack the necessities of life. Ask God to provide for specific needs of which you are aware.

For the Church

Thank God for world missionaries supported by your church. Pray for them by name. Ask God's blessing as they share the Bread of Life in other countries.

For the Kingdom

Picture in your mind scenes of starvation and pain in such places as Somalia, Bosnia, and Romania. Ask God to put an end to fighting and bloodshed. Pray that he will open his hand of spiritual and material blessings on the people of these nations.

For the Unsaved

Pray for new churches which God is using to reach unsaved people all across North America. Pray for their pastors and leaders. Ask for effective outreach into communities and neighborhoods.

Prayer Pointer

"God can pick sense out of a confused prayer." —Richard Sibbes

JUNE 2

Personal Prayer

Praise God for the forgiveness of sins. Give thanks for God's marvelous promise that "if we confess our sins, he is faithful and just and will forgive us our sins and purify us from all unrighteousness" (1 Jn. 1:9). Confess your sins to God. Commit yourself to living in the joyous assurance that your sins are, indeed, forgiven (Ps. 103:3). Ask God to help you sincerely forgive others who have wronged you (Mt. 6:12).

For Your Family and Friends

Every family experiences the effects of sin. Pray that forgiveness will be a common practice in your home and that family members will be quick to forgive offenses both small and large because of Christ.

For the Church

Thank God for those in your congregation who reach out to the disadvantaged. Pray for those who are afflicted in body and soul and for those who care for them.

For the Kingdom

Ask God to ease the tension of racial conflict in our cities and on some campuses. Pray for repentance and forgiveness to heal neighborhoods and communities. Ask God to protect and empower believers who are working for reconciliation.

For the Unsaved

Name one unsaved person you know. Pray that he or she will "repent and be baptized . . . in the name of Jesus Christ" so that his or her sins may be forgiven (Acts 2:38).

JUNE 3

Personal Prayer

Praise God, who is your rock, your fortress, and your deliverer (2 Sam. 22:2). Thank God for delivering you from your sins and for promising to keep you safe from harm even into old age (Isa. 46:4). Confess times when you've played with temptation and not sought God's way out. Commit yourself to living a holy and godly life. Ask God to deliver you from the evil one day by day (Mt. 6:13).

For Your Family and Friends

Pray that Satan will not be able to gain a foothold in the relationships of your family. Ask God to keep the evil of divorce far from your home. Pray for strong marriages among your family and friends.

For the Church

Ask God to pour out his blessing upon the members of your congregation as they give their tithes and offerings each week. Thank God for the opportunity you have to give to his work. Intercede for your deacons.

For the Kingdom

Pray for Christian ministries which help persons with AIDS. Ask God to give them wisdom and grace to reach out to hurting people who have little hope without a cure. Pray for successful AIDS research.

For the Unsaved

God is a God who rescues and saves (Dan. 6:27). Pray that God will rescue and save persons you know who do not yet believe. Ask that they will find God to be the rock, fortress, and deliverer they've been looking for all along.

JUNE 4

Personal Prayer

Praise God as the one who loves you like no one else can. Thank him for loving you "with an everlasting love," drawing you to himself "with loving kindness" (Jer. 31:3). Confess times of presuming upon his love. Commit yourself to reflecting God's love as his image-bearer. Ask him to love others through you, knowing that you can do all things through Christ (Phil. 4:13).

For Your Family and Friends

Pray that God's love will be at least as fully evident in your home as in other relationships. Ask him to regularly prompt you to love your family and friends in ways they can identify.

For the Church

Pray that worship services around the world today will be beautiful reflections of God's love back to him. Ask God to make love a key characteristic of your own congregation.

For the Kingdom

Pray that love for God's ways will prompt you to love mercy (Mic. 6:8) in your societal involvements. Ask God to overcome hatred, violence, and prejudice in your area.

For the Unsaved

Pray that God's people will have so much love for one another that all those around will know they are Jesus' disciples (Jn. 13:35). Ask God to draw the observers to himself through that love.

JUNE 5

Personal Prayer

Praise the one whose control covers even the details of your life (Mt. 6:25-34). Thank God for knowing about your daily needs. Confess any worry. Commit to taking hold of areas where you are to be in charge in your life with the clear knowledge of being "second in command" under God. Ask him for the Spirit's fruit of self-control.

For Your Family and Friends

Pray that God will work self-control into your private life. Ask him to help you be self-controlled with family members and with private disciplines such as eating habits, TV watching, reading materials, time usage, and exercise patterns.

For the Church

Pray that leaders of high-profile ministries and local churches will be men and women of great integrity. Ask God to help them control themselves in temptation, frustration, and other difficulties.

For the Kingdom

Pray that your local, regional, and national government leaders will exercise self-control in fiscal matters as well as other issues of justice. Ask God to strategically place his people in positions of control.

For the Unsaved

Pray that the lack of self-control by some Christians will not effectively barricade non-Christians' receptivity to the good news. Ask the sovereign God to break through barriers to save a particular person in your neighborhood.

JUNE 6

Personal Prayer

Praise your faithful God! Give thanks for God's faithfulness to you even when you are unfaithful to him (2 Tim. 2:11-13). Spend a few minutes asking God to help you think through your life and confessing any unfaithfulness he brings to your attention. Commit yourself as God's image-bearer to reflecting his faithfulness in your own.

For Your Family and Friends

Pray that you and those close to you will be fully faithful—as spouses to marriage vows and as parents to baptismal vows. Ask God to show you how you can encourage such faithfulness.

For the Church

Pray that Christians will be faithful to use individual and corporate outreach opportunities. Ask for the vision to see opportunities and the loving determination to follow through.

For the Kingdom

Pray for opportunities to engage in civic responsibilities. Ask God to help you be effective in service.

For the Unsaved

Pray that faithfulness to one another will draw those who are in the pain of broken marriage vows. Ask God to bring healing and new faithfulness to them through evidences of his healing and faithfulness in your own life.

Prayer Pointer

"We only have to consider the lives of biblical personalities to realize that almost everything they did of kingdom significance followed the exercise of serious prayer." —Gordon MacDonald

JUNE 7

Personal Prayer

Praise God for being sovereign, all-powerful, just, and gentle—all at the same time! Thank him for dealing gently with you in your faults. Confess times of lashing out at others. Commit yourself to reflecting the gentleness of God to those around you, and ask God to produce that part of his Spirit's fruit in abundance in you.

For Your Family and Friends

Pray that you will be consistently gentle with those closest to you. Ask God to help you avoid reactionary responses to family members with habits that annoy you.

For the Church

Pray that gentleness will be a noticeable characteristic of your local church. Ask that those teaching children and new or broken believers be given a special measure of gentleness as they lead.

For the Kingdom

Pray that Christians who differ with one another will present a positive example to the world of how to gently disagree in love. Ask God to present that example also through you in your own conflict situations.

For the Unsaved

Pray that your gentleness will be evident to all (Phil. 4:5). Ask God to use such a witness in the process of saving those near you who are watching your actions.

Prayer Pointer

"No answer to prayer is an indication of our merit; every answer to prayer is an indication of God's mercy." —John Blanchard

JUNE 8

Personal Prayer

Praise God for the joy and peace he brought to the world through Jesus! Thank him for bringing joy and peace to your own life. Ask God to show you any ways you inhibit the joy or peace of others. Confess those ways, as well as any anxiety. Commit yourself to rejoicing continually, handing anxieties to God, and living in the peace which he then gives (Phil. 4:9).

For Your Family and Friends

Pray that you might serve as a peace-maker for those close to you. Ask God to make your home a "safe place," especially for a family member or friend presently in great turmoil.

For the Church

Pray that your local church will be authentically known as a joyful and peaceful people. Ask God to work through world mission efforts to spread true joy and peace to the farthest parts of the earth.

For the Kingdom

Pray that world missionaries working in the midst of spiritual darkness and brokenness will be shining lights of joy and peaceful bearers of God's peace. Ask God to protect them from depression and violence.

For the Unsaved

Pray that the joy and peace of Jesus will draw an unsaved acquaintance to him through you. Ask God to continually produce these parts of the Spirit's fruit in you.

JUNE 9

Personal Prayer

Praise God that he is patient with you, "not wanting anyone to perish, but everyone to come to repentance" (2 Pet. 3:9). Thank God for his patience with you in aspects of life you are slow to let him change. Confess times of presuming upon his patience, and commit yourself to ready and diligent responses to his leading. Ask God to help you, as his image-bearer, to reflect his patience.

For Your Family and Friends

Pray that you and your network of family and friends will remember God's standard: "Love is patient" (1 Cor. 13:4). Ask him to help all of you move that from thought to practice.

For the Church

Pray that all members of your local church will be patient with one another as they minister in the midst of their weaknesses. Ask that fellowship not be broken by impatience or critical spirits.

For the Kingdom

Pray that such patience will also reach out to care for those who are indigent. Ask that patience and wisdom be mixed together to truly assist rather than enable irresponsibility.

For the Unsaved

Pray that you will especially exercise the Spirit's fruit of patience with those who spew their anger at you. Ask God to use that patient love to help them "come to repentance" (2 Pet. 3:9).

JUNE 10

Personal Prayer

Praise God that he is kind and good. Give thanks for specific ways you have experienced that since the beginning of this week. Confess times when you have not been a clear and consistent image-bearer of these characteristics of your God. Commit to reflecting him with such quality that others will praise God for his kindness and goodness shown to them through you. Ask God to produce this part of his Holy Spirit's fruit in you.

For Your Family and Friends

Pray that family members and friends will be kind and good to each other in private as well as in public. Ask God to help them hate what is evil and cling to what is good (Rom. 12:9).

For the Church

Pray that good people in your church will bring good things out of the good stored up in their hearts (Lk. 6:45). Ask God to help members extend this to their financial stewardship.

For the Kingdom

Pray that God's people will honor him by being kind to the needy (Prov. 14:31). Ask God to use those efforts to spread his kingly influence.

For the Unsaved

Pray that God will draw an unsaved person you know to himself with his loving kindness (Jer. 31:3). Ask God to draw that person through his goodness and kindness in you.

JUNE 11

Personal Prayer

Praise God that he is great and greatly to be praised (Ps. 48:1). Give thanks for psalms and hymns that remind us to praise God every day in every activity with which we are involved. Confess your shortcomings in praising God too seldom or too generally. Commit yourself to thanking God for two things every day which you often take for granted. Ask him to help you be a more thanks-living person, joyfully serving him (1 Thess. 5:18).

For Your Family and Friends

Pray that your life may be an example of thanks-living so that family and friends may also give thanks in all things.

For the Church

Pray that your worship this day as well as throughout the week will "extol the LORD at all times, his praise will always be on [your] lips" (Ps. 34:1-2).

For the Kingdom

Pray that thanks-living on the part of every Christian will result in the lessening of racial tension, resolve conflict between peoples and nations, and make even "enemies live at peace with [you]" (Prov. 16:7).

For the Unsaved

Pray for salvation for many seekers as a result of your thanks-living.

Prayer Pointer

"The one concern of the devil is to keep Christians from praying. He fears nothing from prayerless studies, prayerless work, and prayerless religion. He laughs at our toil, mocks at our wisdom, but trembles when we pray."
—Samuel Chadwick

JUNE 12

Personal Prayer

Praise Jesus for his mighty victory over temptation in his confrontation with Satan in the desert (Mt. 4:1-11). Thank God for his promise that you are never tempted beyond what you can handle (1 Cor. 10:13). Confess the many times you have yielded to temptation, not claiming God's power to "resist the devil" (Jas. 4:7). Commit yourself to God that you may overcome evil with good (Prov. 3:7-8). Ask him to assure you that you will overcome all the power of the enemy because of his ultimate victory over Satan at the cross.

For Your Family and Friends

Pray that your family and friends may celebrate your victory over temptation—then feel God's special power for them to be overcomers as well.

For the Church

Pray that the leaders of your church may be real examples of victory over temptation and help others to that end as well.

For the Kingdom

Pray that those in our armed forces will be given extra strength in the face of strong temptation.

For the Unsaved

Pray that you, with the power of God, might use an opportunity today to help an unsaved friend have victory over temptation (Col. 4:5-6).

JUNE 13

Personal Prayer

Praise God for his unsearchable riches in Christ, riches with which nothing can compare (Rom. 11:33-36; Eph. 3:8-12). Thank him for allowing you to share in these riches because of your relationship to Jesus Christ (Col. 2:2-3). Confess your failure to appreciate God's riches and the many times you've looked to what the world calls riches for your happiness. Commit yourself to finding your security in Christ alone. Ask God to help you fully appreciate his riches in Jesus, giving him the glory.

For Your Family and Friends

Pray for opportunities to show God's riches in Christ by some specific act of giving today (Lk. 12:21).

For the Church

Finances are such a big concern in most churches—pray that your church will move forward in faith with outreach ministries it believes God will bless without asking the question "What will it cost?"

For the Kingdom

Pray that the church will give willingly to combat the forces of evil which promote abortion, murder, starvation, etc.

For the Unsaved

Pray that funds will be readily available to further evangelism throughout the world, through such means as church planting, media, local church, crusades, literature, etc.

JUNE 14

Personal Prayer

Praise God for his love for children who often are full of insight (Mk. 10:14-16). Thank God that he teaches you to have a childlike faith (Mt. 11:25). Confess how often you make things so complicated and act so independently of him. Commit yourself to giving out the simple gospel message, "Believe in the Lord Jesus Christ and you will be saved" (Acts 16:31). Ask God to help you recognize every opportunity to have a childlike faith, and not to be childish (Mt. 18:4).

For Your Family and Friends

Pray for all your dear ones to experience that childlike faith, not trying to impress others but to truly be as little children whom Jesus so readily welcomed (Mt. 19:14).

For the Church

Pray that your church will be involved in presenting the gospel simply and sweetly, through the preaching of the Word and the teaching ministry offered for children and adults.

For the Kingdom

Pray that Christians all over the world may "tell the good news" in a childlike way and be ready to welcome all who respond as little children, eager to know more.

For the Unsaved

Pray that your simple acts of love for another will lead you to an opportunity to share the gospel with an unsaved person today.

JUNE 15

Personal Prayer

Praise God that he is greater than all gods—and does what pleases him (Ps. 135:5-6). Give thanks that God has "set apart the godly for himself; . . . [and] hears [you] when [you] call" (Ps. 4:3). Confess your difficulty in accepting that what the Lord does is always good for you or will work out for good (Jer.29:11-14; Rom. 8:28). Commit yourself to spending time with God daily, reading his Word, and claiming these promises for your life. Ask God to keep you faithful as you seek to grow in him.

For Your Family and Friends

Pray for your family and friends to trust God for the wisdom and victory he has available for all as they recognize his greatness (Prov. 2:6-7).

For the Church

Pray that God's greatness will be shown as your church willingly and joyfully supports a specific world missionary with encouragement, prayer, and finances.

For the Kingdom

Pray that God's plan and purpose will not be hindered by threats of Satan and his hosts as God does not want "anyone to perish, but everyone to come to repentance" (2 Pet. 3:9).

For the Unsaved

Pray that the unsaved will recognize the opportune time which God gives them to repent.

JUNE 16

Personal Prayer

Praise God that he wants you to have the full measure of his joy in you as he prayed to his Father in Jn. 17:13. Thank God for filling your heart with joy (Ps. 4:7). Confess any inability to feel "the joy of the LORD is your strength" (Neh. 8:10) due to some situation that may trouble you right now. Commit yourself to reading Paul's letter to the Philippians to inspire you toward greater joy. Ask God to help you be joyful in every situation and to do everything without complaining or arguing (Phil. 2:14).

For Your Family and Friends

Pray that your family and friends may see your joy in the Lord in all situations and likewise be joyful.

For the Church

Pray that God will use you as well as other caregivers in your church to joyfully serve those with special needs today.

For the Kingdom

Pray that God will break down the barriers of hatred within and between nations that cause calamities and problems, by loving and joyful acts which cannot be resisted or denied.

For the Unsaved

Pray that God will use your joy in him to attract your unsaved friends and neighbors and lead you to being a joyful witness for him always (1 Pet. 3:15).

Prayer Pointer

"Prayer is incredibly simple. God answers prayer because his children ask."
—RICHARD FOSTER

JUNE 17

Personal Prayer

Praise God for his wisdom—for your being in Christ Jesus who has become for you wisdom from God! (1 Cor. 1:30, 2:7). Thank God that you may have the full riches of complete understanding to know the mystery of God, namely Christ (Col. 2:2). Confess your lack of understanding. Commit yourself to being wise in the things of God, who makes the wisdom of the world look like foolishness (1 Cor. 1:19-20). Ask God to keep you from being a "wise guy" and to help you lead others to biblical wisdom.

For Your Family and Friends

Pray that God will help you avoid a "holier than thou" attitude with your family and friends (1 Cor. 4:5).

For the Church

Pray for God to give your church and its leaders a real heart for ministry and wisdom to use the resources given in the name of Christ.

For the Kingdom

Pray that Christians will cooperate to resolve many of the issues that separate, rather than unite, neighbors, communities, nations, and peoples, in the love of Jesus.

For the Unsaved

Pray for wisdom to show a specific act of kindness today to an unsaved neighbor.

JUNE 18

Personal Prayer

Praise God as the one to whom you have given your entire life. Thank him for desiring to be Lord of everything that you have and are, and for asking nothing less. Confess those parts of your life that you still hold back from God's complete authority. Commit yourself to laying these areas before God throughout the day, looking for his help in surrendering them completely. Ask God to help you be completely devoted to him and his will (Col. 3:17).

For Your Family and Friends

Pray that God will help young adults that you know become willing to give their lives completely for him and the gospel.

For the Church

Ask that your church's worship be made uplifting not only by music and preaching but also by the sacrificial lives of members who have served Christ during the week (Rom. 12:1).

For the Kingdom

Pray that throughout the world, worship will lift up the name of Jesus and defeat the forces of Satan.

For the Unsaved

Pray that the unsaved who visit church services in your city this week will be struck with the genuineness of believers' worship and the power of the Word in their lives (1 Cor. 14:24-25).

JUNE 19

Personal Prayer

Give praise to the one who has created love, the one who is the very heart and nature of love (1 Jn. 4:16). Thank God for his love for you—a deeply personal love that will never let you go (Rom. 8:38-39). Confess those times when you have been unable to receive and return God's love for you this past week. Commit yourself to meditating daily on God's strong love for you. Ask him to fill you with the knowledge of his love, so that you may be filled with the fullness of God (Eph. 3:17-19).

For Your Family and Friends

Pray for those marriages where love is failing, that God will miraculously restore the ability to forgive, to cherish, and to receive each other with affection.

For the Church

Pray that your congregation will be so saturated and overwhelmed with a sense of God's love that you will reach out to your neighborhood with a love that is unmistakably Christlike.

For the Kingdom

Ask God for leaders who embody love in every way, putting aside ambition and pride to serve others (Phil. 2:3).

For the Unsaved

Pray that Christ will show his love through you to one unsaved person today.

Prayer Pointer

"God shapes the world by prayer. Prayers are deathless. They outlive the lives of those who utter them."—E. M. Bounds

JUNE 20

Personal Prayer

Praise God as the high and lofty One who lives forever, who lives in a high and holy place, but also with those who are contrite and lowly in spirit (Isa. 57:15). Thank him for choosing the lowliness of the cross to show his power and wisdom to the world (1 Cor. 1:20-25). Confess any resistance on your part to sharing in the humility of the gospel. Commit yourself to laying your pride daily before the feet of Christ. Ask Jesus to help you empty yourself in service to God, as he did (Philippians 2).

For Your Family and Friends

Pray against any rifts between family members that you know of, that the spirit of pride may be defeated and relationships be restored in a spirit of humility and love.

For the Church

Ask that your church's outreach ministries be done in a spirit of humility that sees the beauty of Jesus in everyone who is served (Mt. 25:34-40).

For the Kingdom

Pray that the leaders of your country will be given the humility to seek wisdom and strength from God for their tasks.

For the Unsaved

Ask God to break down the spiritual blindness of unsaved friends, enabling them to see the power and wisdom of the cross.

JUNE 21

Personal Prayer

Give glory and honor to God as one whose wisdom and knowledge are too vast and deep ever to be grasped by the human mind. Thank the Father for having revealed himself in human, finite form in his Son, Jesus (Jn. 14:7). Confess the times during this week when you have failed to look to Jesus for help in understanding the Father's heart and mind. Commit yourself daily to prayer for this understanding (Eph. 1:17). Ask God to open the eyes of your heart as you look to Jesus and study his life and words in the gospels.

For Your Family and Friends

Commit your immediate family members to the wisdom of God, remembering that God's ways are past understanding and claiming that God will work all things for their good (Rom. 8:28).

For the Church

Pray that your church education teachers will not limit God's Word to simple formulas but will also teach children awe at the splendor, glory, and unsearchable wisdom of God in Jesus.

For the Kingdom

Pray for those who speak of God's Word on the radio and television, that they may clearly present the wisdom of the cross to those whose minds are darkened (1 Cor. 2:11-14).

For the Unsaved

Ask for wisdom in explaining the cross of Christ to an unsaved friend or acquaintance this week.

JUNE 22

Personal Prayer

Magnify God as the one whose Word will outlive this world (Isa. 40:8). Thank Jesus that he is coming again to establish a new heavens and earth, at an hour that the Father has set (Mt. 24:30-31, 36). Confess those times when you let this perspective slip out of your daily life and prayers. Commit yourself daily to setting your hope and expectation on Jesus' coming again. Ask God to show you what you must do in the time that you have left (24:45-51).

For Your Family and Friends

Pray for the homes you know that are nominally Christian, that God would set their hearts on fire and may show them the urgency of his kingdom work.

For the Church

Pray that the members of your congregation would join with other churches in your neighborhood as they see how large the harvest is and how many workers are still needed to reach the unsaved around you (Mt. 9:37-38).

For the Kingdom

Ask God's Spirit to give clear leading to those who are considering his call to world missions. Examine your heart also to see what God may be asking of you in this area.

For the Unsaved

Ask God to show you the urgency of the gospel message and to give you the opportunity to share it with someone today.

JUNE 23

Personal Prayer

Praise God as one who is perfect in power and judgment but also perfect in mercy and kindness. Give thanks for God's mercy to you (Eph. 2:4-5). Confess your inability to show mercy as completely and graciously as your Father does. Commit yourself to living with a greater awareness of God's mercy and kindness in your life (Eph. 1:7-8). Ask God to extend this grace to others who have irritated or hurt you.

For Your Family and Friends

Ask God to give you the power to extend forgiveness and mercy to family members or acquaintances with whom you have a broken relationship.

For the Church

Pray that those in your church who struggle with guilt and an inability to forgive will be changed by an awareness of God's great and free mercy toward them in Jesus. Pray for wisdom for your pastor, elders, and others who counsel these people.

For the Kingdom

Ask God to make his church worldwide a shining example of people who extend mercy and kindness even to their enemies (Mt. 5:44-45).

For the Unsaved

Intercede for your unsaved friends and acquaintances, that God would put in their hearts a hunger for his mercy and forgiveness.

Prayer Pointer

"All who have walked with God have viewed prayer as the main business of their lives." —Delma Jackson

JUNE 24

Personal Prayer

Glorify God as the all-sufficient one, who through his limitless power fills everything in every way (Eph. 1:23). Thank God for giving you his Spirit to meet all your needs as you do his will. Confess those times you have sought fulfillment in ways which did not honor God. Commit your needs to him (Phil. 4:19). Ask God for a greater awareness of his power to help you grow spiritually (2 Pet. 1:3-8).

For Your Family and Friends

Pray for friends who struggle with material or spiritual poverty. Ask God to help them understand that he can meet both areas of need with his riches in Christ.

For the Church

Intercede for your deacons in their work of mercy, that they will be moved to pray daily for God's provision, recognizing him as the source of their funds and their desire to help others.

For the Kingdom

Ask that God will use you and others in your congregation to answer the desperate pleas for help and funds from kingdom ministries (2 Cor. 9:10-14).

For the Unsaved

Pray that no nation, city, or person will go without hearing the gospel simply because there was not enough money given to support evangelists and preachers.

JUNE 25

Personal Prayer

Praise God for his quietness, restoration, and strength (Ps. 23:2-3). Give thanks that God will give you that quiet time to reflect on his restoring power and quietness (Ps. 46:10). Confess your failure to be still before the Lord so he can speak to you. Commit yourself to a daily time of worship and adoration of God. Ask God for assurance that in quietness and trust is your strength (Isa. 30:15).

For Your Family and Friends

Pray that your family and friends would "rejoice in the Lord always" (Phil. 4:4) as they realize that God quiets us with his love (Zeph. 3:17).

For the Church

Pray that the church will not be silent, but will spread the Word of God in mighty ways today, even as Jesus told the Pharisees in Lk. 19:40 that "if they keep quiet, the stones will cry out."

For the Kingdom

Pray that God's kingdom will prosper as his servants lead the way in having "the unfading beauty of a gentle and quiet spirit, which is of great worth in God's sight" (1 Pet. 3:4).

For the Unsaved

Pray that your quietness before God will result in winning the "respect of outsiders" (1 Thess. 4:11-12) so that they will see Jesus in you.

JUNE 26

Personal Prayer

Praise God for his leadership over the redeemed because of his unfailing love and strength (Ex. 15:11, 13). Give thanks for leaders who speak the Word of God to you (Heb. 13:7). Confess your lack of recognizing God's leadership through others that he brings into your life and your failure to support them with your prayers (1 Tim. 2:1-2). Commit yourself to following God's leadership as he brings you into a land "flowing with milk and honey" (Num. 14:8). Ask God to help you be a good leader in bringing others to him.

For Your Family and Friends

Pray that your family members and friends may accept the leadership you offer, leading many to righteousness and shining like the stars as stated in Dan. 12:3.

For the Church

Pray for church leaders to depend on God for skills that will be recognized by others and used for God's glory.

For the Kingdom

Pray that all would obey their leaders and submit to their authority (Heb. 13:17) so their work will be a joy.

For the Unsaved

Ask that all Christians will "walk the walk" and not just "talk the talk" that will lead others to salvation in Jesus.

Prayer Pointer

"The power of the promise 'Ask, and it will be given you' lies in the loving relationship between us as children and God as our Father." —Maxie Dunnam

JUNE 27

Personal Prayer

Praise God for his strength and confidence, enduring from everlasting to everlasting (1 Chron. 29:10-11). Give thanks that God is your strength and confidence and that he will never fail you or forsake you (1 Chron. 28:20). Confess to the Lord your failure to rely completely upon him and his Word (Isa. 41:10). Commit yourself to being strong and doing the work God has for you without complaining (Phil. 2:14). Ask God to forgive you for not depending on him and that you may wait on the Lord and be confident of his love (Jeremiah 31:3).

For Your Family and Friends

Pray that your family and friends would also claim the strength and peace that God gives to his people (Ps. 29:11).

For the Church

Pray that your church will be strong in preparing its membership to grow in their daily walk and work for him as parents, teachers, workers, etc.

For the Kingdom

Pray that God's kingdom will prosper as we all move forward in his strength and confidence—not on our own!

For the Unsaved

Pray that your unsaved friends and neighbors will benefit from your confidence in God as you speak to them about it—and come to know God personally as a result (1 Pet. 3:15).

JUNE 28

Personal Prayer

Praise God for being the great healer who gives real peace and security for you to enjoy (Jer. 33:6). Give thanks for the many miraculous healings that show God's power at work. Confess your failure to appreciate the health God gives you and your complaining when things aren't going well (Ps. 139:23). Commit yourself to praising God each day for a healthy body, for legs and arms, fingers and toes, eyes and ears—a body that functions so beautifully. Ask him for guidance in blessing him at all times even if these body parts aren't always working right (Ps. 34:1).

For Your Family and Friends

Pray for family members and friends who are not experiencing good health. Praise him for accepting your prayers (Ps. 6:9).

For the Church

Pray for your church to be very compassionate and able to minister to those who do not experience good health, have disabilities, or have met with serious accident.

For the Kingdom

Pray for God's kingdom to advance in meaningful ways as you seek new means to reach out to the "sin-sick" people of the world (Mt. 9:13).

For the Unsaved

Pray for the unsaved to see that "it is not the healthy who need a doctor but the sick" (9:12)—to see their "sick" condition and come to Jesus' open arms of love.

JUNE 29

Personal Prayer

Praise God that he is in control of every storm (Mk. 4:35-39). Thank him that he does not want anyone to perish but to have everlasting life in him (2 Pet. 3:9). Confess to God your wrong response to the stormy, unexpected events in your life that leave you feeling panicky and fretful. Commit every stormy situation, as well as every good one, to God as he cares for you, restores you, and makes you strong (1 Pet. 5:7, 10). Ask God to calm any anxiety or fear that you are experiencing.

For Your Family and Friends

Pray for your family and friends to experience real calm in their lives, to be carefree and not afraid, to stand firm in the Lord as Isaiah was reminded in Isa. 7:4, 9.

For the Church

Pray for the needs, fears, and storms encountered in the daily lives of missionary families.

For the Kingdom

Pray that God's kingdom will prosper as Christians spread the words of Ps. 107:29, "[God] stills the storms to a whisper . . . he guide[s] them to their desired haven. Let them give thanks to the LORD for his unfailing love."

For the Unsaved

Pray for troubled unbelievers to find victory over stormy lives in the calm that only Jesus can give.

JUNE 30

Personal Prayer

Praise God for his plans, from all eternity, done in perfect faithfulness (Isa. 25:1) which will come to pass as he purposes (Isa. 14:24). Thank God for his plans for you—to prosper you and not to harm you, to give you hope and a future (Jer. 29:11). Confess to him your failure to learn contentment in every situation as Paul did (Phil. 4:11). Commit yourself to fearing the Lord, which leads to life, and thus rest content, untouched by trouble (Prov. 19:23). Ask God for real contentment in what you have (Heb. 13:5), remembering that he will never fail you nor forsake you.

For Your Family and Friends

Pray that your family and friends will obey and serve the Lord and thus spend their years in contentment (Job 36:11).

For the Church

Pray that your church will experience real contentment, that internal problems will be resolved so real caregiving will be ongoing!

For the Kingdom

Pray that God will challenge you to be involved in some kingdom endeavor close to home such as an assistance ministry. Ask God to give you real satisfaction in helping others.

For the Unsaved

Pray that your contentment in a difficult situation God has placed you in may result in the salvation of an unsaved friend.

Prayer Pointer

"Men May spurn our appeals, reject our message, oppose our arguments, despise our persons, but they are helpless against our prayers." —Sidlow Baxter

JULY 1

Personal Prayer

Praise God for being the God of all creation (Gen. 1:31). Thank God for the variety in his creation, in plants and animals, and especially in people (Rom. 12:4-6). Confess to him your lack of appreciation for so many of the things he has done and made (1 Tim. 4:4-5). Commit each day to the Lord, showing special appreciation for one thing in nature that you've not noticed in the past. Ask God to help you be more observant as you are involved in your daily activities, praising him abundantly (Ps. 135).

For Your Family and Friends

Pray that your appreciation of little things will help your family and friends be more appreciative of the beauty of God's creation (Psalm 148).

For the Church

Pray that your church leaders may take a greater stand in teaching everyone to respect and take care of God's beautiful creation.

For the Kingdom

Pray that you may be concerned about your environment and make a difference in the pollution problems that face our world today.

For the Unsaved

Ask that you will be an example in doing your part in cleaning up your world—and that God will use that as an opportunity to witness to the unsaved.

JULY 2

Personal Prayer

Praise God as the one worthy of the worship of our entire lives (Rom. 12:1-2). Give thanks for God's mercy shown to you personally. Confess times of conforming to the pattern of this world. Commit yourself to the continual renewing of your mind. Ask God to be true to his promise that you will be able to test and approve what is his will.

For Your Family and Friends

Pray that your household and friends will be excellent worshipers in church services. Ask God to lead you from special worship times to the worship of daily devotion to him throughout the week.

For the Church

Pray for God to move in special ways throughout the world upon his gathered people. Ask him to help members remember that they belong to each other (12:5).

For the Kingdom

Pray that each of God's people will be reminded of the different gifts he or she possesses, according to the grace of God (12:6). Ask that they be further equipped through worship to use those gifts for God's kingdom (12:7ff.).

For the Unsaved

Ask God to love people to himself through your words and actions.

JULY 3

Personal Prayer

Praise God for meeting with his people in special ways through weekly worship services. Give thanks that you can continue to be with him today! Confess times of ignoring God during the weekdays. Commit yourself to a special time of worshiping God through personal devotions each day this week. Ask the Lord to remind you of his presence throughout this day.

For Your Family and Friends

Pray that you and those close to you may faithfully apply what God showed all of you through pastors and teachers in Sunday's worship. Ask God to help you be humble and gentle in this, encouraging each other rather than being judgmental.

For the Church

Pray for your local and international church leaders as they do their work this week. Ask God to prompt them to diligent use of their leadership gifts and positions (Rom. 12:8).

For the Kingdom

Pray especially for leaders of God's church who are highly visible through the news media. Ask God to give them humble courage and a consistently brilliant witness.

For the Unsaved

Pray that unsaved persons around the world will see that brilliant witness of Christian leaders and glorify God. Ask God to shine clearly and consistently through you in your sphere of influence.

JULY 4

Personal Prayer

Praise God verbally, saying, "Jesus is Lord" (Rom. 10:9). Thank Christ for fulfilling God's law for you and granting you his righteousness (10:4). Confess any attempts you are still making to earn righteousness and favor with God. Commit to a lifestyle of confessing the lordship of Jesus. Ask God to remove any lingering distrust (10:11).

For Your Family and Friends

Pray one by one for every member of your household to call on the name of the Lord and be saved (10:13). Ask God to help them believe through your witness.

For the Church

Pray for joyful and obedient involvement in the outreach ministries sponsored by your local church and your denomination. Ask God to give real wisdom to those involved in planning strategies to enable God's people to be more and more effective.

For the Kingdom

Pray for God's kingdom to come and his will to be done on your part of the earth as it is in heaven. Ask that the lordship of Christ, which we confess verbally, will be applied in just and righteous actions.

For the Unsaved

Thank God for those specially gifted and dedicated to bringing the good news (10:15). Ask him to use you in going and sending others (10:14).

Prayer Pointer

"Daily prayers lessen daily cares." —Anonymous

JULY 5

Personal Prayer

Praise God for the depth of the riches of his wisdom and knowledge (Rom. 11:33). Give thanks that "from him and through him and to him are all things" (11:36). Confess times of thinking that God owes you favors or explanations (11:35). Commit yourself to thinking deeply about God until you come to the end of your ability to understand. Ask God to help you reach that point with wonder and amazement rather than doubt or cynicism (11:33-36).

For Your Family and Friends

Pray that the education of the children of your family and friends leads them to marvel at God's greatness. Ask God for teachers acutely aware of his design and involvement in all areas of creation.

For the Church

Pray for your church's educational program and personnel. Ask that God's church will also be faithful in supporting Christian education beyond its local ministries.

For the Kingdom

Pray that God will help all believers to be students of his ways with eyes to see and minds to understand more of his caring control. Ask that God's kingdom will soon come in fullness.

For the Unsaved

Pray for those who do not understand from a God-centered perspective. Ask God to open their hearts to his Word.

JULY 6

Personal Prayer

Praise God as the one who will soon crush Satan under your feet (Rom. 16:20). Thank him for revealing the mysteries of his salvation to you (16:25-27). Asking God to show you your sin, confess any ways in which you have been involved in causing divisions in Christ's people or have put up obstacles that impeded the spread of his Word (16:17-18). Commit yourself to being "wise about what is good, and innocent about what is evil" (16:19).

For Your Family and Friends

Pray for your family and friends to be personally involved in reaching the world for Christ. Ask God for a world-sized vision which also has your immediate neighborhood in view.

For the Church

Pray for workers to go into the harvest fields of the world. Ask God to prompt his people to abundant contributions of finances, prayer, and encouragement to send these missionaries.

For the Kingdom

Pray for cooperation between Christian denominations and mission personnel. Ask God to help believers seek his kingdom and righteousness above the growth of their own ministries.

For the Unsaved

Pray for the nations to believe and obey God, asking him to establish both "new" and "old" believers through the proclamation of Jesus Christ (16:26).

JULY 7

Personal Prayer

Praise God for his excellence in creation. Give thanks for the creation's variety and splendor. Confess ways in which you have misused parts of it. Commit yourself to the proper care and use of God's creation. Ask God to help you regard it as "clean" (Rom. 14:14), receiving it from him with thanksgiving.

For Your Family and Friends

Pray for healing for any family member or friend who is misusing drugs, alcohol, nicotine, or any other part of creation. Ask God to bring conviction of needed changes through his Spirit.

For the Church

Pray for sensitivity among Christians toward one another's beliefs about food, drink, religious observances, and other discretionary matters (Romans 14), so that fellowship and caring might not be hindered. Ask God to help you to "make every effort to do what leads to peace and to mutual edification" (14:19).

For the Kingdom

Pray that the world will be attracted by the loving care Christians show one another instead of being repulsed by in-fighting. Ask God to move his church to compassionate caring and healing without compromising his truth and methods.

For the Unsaved

Pray for anyone in your circle of contacts who is hurting. Ask God to show you a specific way in which you can show his care to that person or family.

JULY 8

Personal Prayer

Praise God as the one who again has supplied you with all you have needed this week. Thank him for putting some of his resources into your care. Confess any waste or mismanagement of those resources this week. Commit yourself to sharing with God's people who are in need (Rom. 12:13). Ask God to bring to mind the name of someone with whom he would have you share by showing hospitality (12:13).

For Your Family and Friends

Pray that your children and those of your friends learn principles of Christian stewardship from an early age. Ask God to make you an excellent example for them.

For the Church

Pray that those entrusted with the special spiritual gift of contributing to the needs of others will give generously (12:8). Ask God to give you and all members of your church a desire to lay up their treasures in heaven (Mt. 6:20).

For the Kingdom

Pray that God will keep prompting his people to overflow with love and good deeds. Ask that such generous love will result in people praising the Father in heaven (Mt. 5:16).

For the Unsaved

Pray for Christian missions to be so generously supported that they can focus on evangelism instead of fund-raising. Ask God to multiply their resources and effectiveness, bringing many into his family.

JULY 9

Personal Prayer

Praise God for his everlasting love (Jer. 31:3), which has no end. Thank God for demonstrating his love for you by sending his Son to die in your place (Rom. 5:8). Confess any lack of love you have experienced toward God or other believers. Commit yourself to bearing the fruit of love by the power of the Holy Spirit (Gal. 5:22). Ask God to enable you daily to "put on love" (Col. 3:14).

For Your Family and Friends

Thank God for the love of your family and friends. Pray for any unbelieving friends or family members that they will experience the saving love of Christ (Eph. 2:4-5).

For the Church

As you gather with other believers for worship this week, pray that "being rooted and established in love . . . [you may] grasp how wide and long and high and deep is the love of Christ" (Eph. 3:17-18). Let this thought flood your mind in worship.

For the Kingdom

Ask that love will characterize the relationships of believers throughout the world and in your own denomination. Pray that the virtues of faith, hope, and love will be evident, but that love will be preeminent.

For the Unsaved

Think of one unsaved person. Name that individual and ask God to reveal his redeeming love in Christ in that person's life. Pray for an opportunity this week to share the good news.

JULY 10

Personal Prayer

Rejoice with the prophet Isaiah, who wrote, "I delight greatly in the LORD; my soul rejoices in my God. For he has clothed me with garments of salvation and arrayed me in a robe of righteousness" (Isa. 61:10). Thank God for producing such joy in your life. Confess any lack of Christian joy. Commit yourself to bearing the fruit of joy through the power of the Holy Spirit (Gal. 5:22). Ask God to fill you with an inexpressible and glorious joy (1 Pet. 1:8).

For Your Family and Friends

Pray for joy to fill your home. Ask God to root out anything that will rob your family of enjoying each other.

For the Church

Are your church leaders joyful persons? Pray that they will be so in their family life and work in the church. Pray especially that your pastor(s) will be "overtaken" with gladness and joy (Isa. 35:10).

For the Kingdom

Sin causes much gloom and sadness to blanket our world. Ask God to spare the church in every country from such sorrow. Pray that the church's joy will shine like a beacon light to those who are oppressed and joyless.

For the Unsaved

Pray for your own expression of joy in the Lord. Do unbelievers recognize it in you? Do they know the source of your joy? Ask God to make your joy genuinely contagious.

JULY 11

Personal Prayer

Praise the one who came as the Prince of Peace (Isa. 9:6). Thank Jesus for giving peace to his beloved ones (Jn. 14:27). Confess those times when you've allowed Satan to fill your soul with unrest. Commit yourself to bearing the fruit of peace by the power of the Holy Spirit (Gal. 5:22). Ask God to guard your heart and mind today with his peace (Phil. 4:7).

For Your Family and Friends

Peace is such a rare commodity in families today. Ask God to bring his peace into all of your family relationships. Pray also for peace among your friends.

For the Church

Intercede today for outreach ministries in your church or community which take the love of Christ into your neighborhood. Ask that their work will be richly blessed.

For the Kingdom

Warfare, bloodshed, strife, and turmoil mar every corner of the globe these days. But the good news is that Christ came "to reconcile to himself all things . . . by making peace through his blood, shed on the cross" (Col. 1:20). Pray for all those who seek to bring Christ's reconciliation to a restless world.

For the Unsaved

Pray for specific unsaved neighbors, that they will be justified by faith and enjoy eternal peace with God through Jesus Christ (Rom. 5:1).

JULY 12

Personal Prayer

Praise God for his patience. Thank the Lord for being patient with you and allowing you to come to repentance in Christ (2 Pet. 3:9). Confess impatience you have felt or expressed toward God or other people. Commit yourself to bearing the fruit of patience through the power of the Holy Spirit (Gal. 5:22). Ask God to fill you with his patience.

For Your Family and Friends

If you have small children, you know how quickly impatient words can surface in families. Pray for families who struggle with showing patience among family members.

For the Church

Remember the education committee of your church today. Pray for teachers, helpers, and learners in your education ministry. Pray especially for growth in your adult education classes.

For the Kingdom

Impatience is a hallmark of our me-first society. Pray that the church will have a softening influence, proclaiming and demonstrating a patient "Jesus-first" message. Ask that the church will be patient even in the midst of affliction (Rom. 12:12).

For the Unsaved

Claim God's promise toward the unsaved in 2 Pet. 3:9. While thanking God for his patience, pray that his salvation will be made known to many unbelieving people today.

Prayer Pointer

"A man prayed, and at first he thought that prayer was talking. But he became more and more quiet until in the end he realized that prayer was listening."
—Søren Kierkegaard

JULY 13

Personal Prayer

Praise the God of everlasting kindness (Isa. 54:8). Thank him for exercising kindness, justice, and righteousness—and for delighting in them (Jer. 9:24). Confess any unkind deed or word or thought that has hurt another person. Commit yourself to bearing the fruit of kindness by the power of the Holy Spirit (Gal. 5:22). Ask God to add kindness to your faith (2 Pet. 1:5-7).

For Your Family and Friends

Ask God to help your family members and friends show kindness in all their relationships. Pray that kind words and deeds will become common in your household (Eph. 4:32).

For the Church

Pray for the outreach of your congregation and denomination to unbelievers in other countries. Ask that in all their gospel work, missionaries will be clothed with compassion, kindness, humility, gentleness, and patience (Col. 3:12).

For the Kingdom

Ask God to uphold Christian agencies which do kind deeds in the name of Christ for impoverished and hungry people. Pray that needs will be met for both giver and receiver.

For the Unsaved

Pray that your kind attitude will attract unsaved friends and coworkers to the Lord. Ask God to create natural opportunities for you to share your faith.

JULY 14

Personal Prayer

Praise God for his marvelous goodness. Thank the Lord for being a refuge in times of trouble (Nah. 1:7). Confess your own failure to show goodness toward others. Commit yourself to bearing the fruit of goodness through the power of the Holy Spirit (Gal. 5:22). Ask God to enable you today to "taste and see that the LORD is good" (Ps. 34:8).

For Your Family and Friends

Pray for goodness to be evident in the lives of your family members and friends. Ask God to help each one to imitate the goodness of God.

For the Church

Intercede for individuals and groups in your congregation who reach out to persons "on the fringe" and promote Christian fellowship. Ask that the good which they do will be an example for others to follow.

For the Kingdom

Pray that good will win out over evil in every area of our society. Ask that righteousness and justice will permeate the fabric of our culture so that God will be glorified and praised.

For the Unsaved

Ask for an opportunity today to do good for an unbelieving friend. Pray that God will turn that encounter into a conversation of "good news."

Prayer Pointer

"Prayer is spoken of more often than any other activity of the gathered [New Testament] church."—KENT R. WILSON

JULY 15

Personal Prayer

Praise your covenant God for his abiding faithfulness (Deut. 7:9). Give thanks that even "if we are faithless, he will remain faithful" (2 Tim. 2:13). Confess any unfaithfulness you've allowed into your relationships with God and others. Commit yourself to bearing the fruit of faithfulness through the power of the Holy Spirit (Gal. 5:22). Ask God to help you be a faithful follower of Jesus Christ.

For Your Family and Friends

Pray that God's covenant love would extend through your generation and on to generations yet to come.

For the Church

Thank God for those in your congregation who evidence faithfulness in their financial management and liberal giving. Praise God for dedicated deacons who exercise responsible and godly stewardship in your church.

For the Kingdom

Pray that the church, Christ's body here on earth, will remain faithful to the Word and obedient to the Spirit. When persecution comes, ask that believers will "commit themselves to their faithful Creator and continue to do good" (1 Pet. 4:19).

For the Unsaved

Ask God to help you to be a faithful witness as he gives you opportunity in your everyday routine. Pray that in your relationships with unsaved people God will "strengthen and protect you from the evil one" (2 Thess. 3:3).

JULY 16

Personal Prayer

In your heart sing to the Lord, your strength and song; praise the one who has become your salvation. Give thanks that with joy you can draw water from the wells of salvation (Isa. 12:2-3). Confess that your worship is sometimes lacking because you don't always remember the greatness of your salvation. Commit yourself to worshiping and singing with your whole heart; ask God to make you awake and alive to the power of his Word and the joy of music.

For Your Family and Friends

Ask God to minister to hurting family members or friends through the Word and through the supportive, caring comments of other church members.

For the Church

Pray for families with young children and teenagers, that the children may feel a sense of participation in worship this week and of belonging to the body of Christ.

For the Kingdom

Pray that worship may unite a "great multitude that no one could count, from every nation, tribe, people and language" in praise of the God of our salvation and the Lamb who sits upon the throne (Rev. 7:9-10).

For the Unsaved

Ask the Spirit to draw the unsaved on your street to a church where they can find hope and healing in the preaching of God's Word.

JULY 17

Personal Prayer

Give praise to the one by whom all things were created, the one in whom all things hold together, the head of the church (Col. 1:16-18). Thank God for giving direction and purpose to your life in this day. Confess those times in the past few weeks when you've tried to take over the direction of your life. Commit yourself completely to Christ's leadership in this week. Ask him to help you find the time to listen for his voice at the beginning of each day.

For Your Family and Friends

Pray for those close to you who are struggling with finding some direction in their lives. Commit yourself to encouraging them to seek God's will.

For the Church

Intercede for the leaders in your congregation, that they may find the wisdom and courage to follow Christ's plan for your church without hesitating.

For the Kingdom

Ask the Spirit to guide church leaders in war-torn countries, that they may know what work Jesus has for their churches amid the ethnic tensions and political struggles of their people.

For the Unsaved

Pray that God will use your maturity in Christ to provide leadership for someone whose life is out of control and in need of spiritual direction.

JULY 18

Personal Prayer

Praise the Lord Jesus, who will be "revealed from heaven in blazing fire with his powerful angels" (2 Thess. 1:7). Thank him that he will come to restore justice and righteousness in the earth. Confess the times when you have not lived in awareness of Christ's coming again in power and judgment. Ask him to help you desire and look forward to his coming, and commit yourself to preparing yourself and others for "the day he comes to be glorified in his holy people and to be marveled at among all who have believed" (1:10).

For Your Family and Friends

Pray daily for the salvation of any family members or close friends whose lives show that they do not truly believe that Christ is coming in power and judgment.

For the Church

Ask the Spirit to give the churches in your community a sense of urgency in bringing the good news of Jesus' death and resurrection to the unchurched and unbelieving in their neighborhoods.

For the Kingdom

Pray for the protection of Jesus' blood and the power of his cross over all North American missionaries who are working to reclaim those blinded by New Age religion, by materialism, or by drugs or sex addiction.

For the Unsaved

Ask God to change the hearts of those who don't love the truth, and to set them free from Satan's lies.

JULY 19

Personal Prayer

Praise the Son of God, in whom are hidden all the treasures of wisdom and knowledge. Thank God for the depth of the riches of that wisdom and knowledge (Rom. 11:33). Confess those areas of your work or personal life for which you have forgotten to ask his wisdom and guidance. Commit yourself to calling out for insight and crying aloud for understanding, to looking for it as for silver and searching for it as for hidden treasure (Prov. 2:3). Ask God to let his discretion protect you and his understanding guard you.

For Your Family and Friends

Intercede for the parents you know who are struggling with raising their children, that God will open their hearts to his wisdom.

For the Church

Pray for the adult education classes at your church, that many more adults will be drawn to see that there is much more they can learn from the storehouse of God's wisdom.

For the Kingdom

Ask God's Spirit to equip and support those who are training Christian leaders from among tribes and peoples who have no previous Bible knowledge or background.

For the Unsaved

Claim the power of God in your unsaved acquaintances' lives to break down the strongholds of ignorance and to win them to the "foolishness" of the cross—the power and wisdom of God.

JULY 20

Personal Prayer

Praise the God who knows the depths of your heart and sees all the secret places there. Give thanks that he hears the prayers of many people all over the earth and listens to all of our cries for help. Confess to God the days in this past week when you have not made sufficient time for prayer for yourself and others. Commit yourself to remembering his deep love for you and all people, and ask the Spirit to make that awareness grow into a habit of praying without ceasing "on all occasions with all kinds of prayers and requests" (Eph. 6:18).

For Your Family and Friends

Ask God to cause the parents you know to pray daily for their children, relying on God's protection and saving grace in their lives.

For the Church

Lift up to God the names of the world missionaries your church supports, asking that their specific needs for this day may be met.

For the Kingdom

Pray for the governments of countries in war or civil strife, that they may protect the missionaries and other Christians who are working for Christ within their borders.

For the Unsaved

Ask God to hear and answer the prayers of the unsaved, "so that all peoples of the earth may know [his] name and fear [him]" (1 Ki. 8:43). as a God who listens and responds.

JULY 21

Personal Prayer

Glorify the Lord, who is gracious, full of compassion, and gentle with the weak (Ps. 116:5). Thank God for rescuing you during those times when you needed his help, even when you didn't ask for it (116:8). Confess the times when you have been impatient with others in need. Commit yourself to remembering throughout this day God's compassion for you and to reflecting that compassion to others. Ask God to help you fulfill this vow.

For Your Family and Friends

Intercede for those you know who are "overcome by trouble and sorrow" (116:3), that God will move them to call on his name and to rely on his compassionate help.

For the Church

Ask God to make the congregations in your community centers of kindness, where those in need will find the hands of Jesus ministering to them.

For the Kingdom

Pray for prison officials, that their administration of justice and punishment may be tempered with compassion and kindness.

For the Unsaved

Ask God to use your friendship with one unsaved person this week as a bridge to showing him or her the gracious love of God.

Prayer Pointer

"Prayer is the great engine to overthrow and rout my spiritual enemies, the great means to procure the graces of which I stand in hourly need." —John Newton

JULY 22

Personal Prayer

Glorify God as the one who fills all of your desires and needs with his presence alone. Thank God for being sufficient for you even when every other source of joy or support is taken away. Confess your dependence on other people or situations to make you content and happy. Commit yourself to making Jesus your "pearl of great price," and ask him to make you willing to give up all you have for the sake of his kingdom, if necessary (Mt. 13:44-46).

For Your Family and Friends

Pray that God will lead them into a life-style that reflects a love for God, not a love for things.

For the Church

Ask God to pour his blessings especially on those members who, like the poor widow, are giving their very last dollar so that God's work can be accomplished in your neighborhood.

For the Kingdom

Pray for the hunger, agriculture, and disaster relief organizations around the world, that they may use the funds given them to the best possible ends.

For the Unsaved

Ask God to bring to your mind the material needs of an unsaved acquaintance so that you will be able to help meet those needs and bring that person closer to the kingdom.

JULY 23

Personal Prayer

Praise God for not leaving you "as orphans" but for giving another helper to be with you forever (Jn. 14:16, 18). Give thanks for God's presence and power, and trust him to continue to energize you, keeping you on the right course. Confess the times you are dissatisfied or frustrated in your walk with the Lord. Commit yourself anew to God and let his Spirit help you in your weakness, especially in prayer (Rom. 8:26). Ask him to reveal himself to you today in a new and fresh way.

For Your Family and Friends

Pray that your family and friends will have the joy, peace, and stability that comes from knowing God personally and spending time daily with him (Col. 3:15-17).

For Your Church

Pray for your church to excel in gifts that build it up by the enabling power of the Holy Spirit, demonstrated by effective preaching and fellowship that brings growth and harmony (1 Cor. 14:12).

For the Kingdom

Pray that the enabling power of the Holy Spirit will bring the coming of God's kingdom all over the world, beginning right where you are now (Acts 1:8).

For the Unsaved

Pray that the true witness of Christians in the "marketplace" will draw all people to Jesus (Jn. 12:32).

JULY 24

Personal Prayer

Praise God for being the God of "burning bushes," calling you to respond and serve where he leads (Ex. 3:2). Thank God for revealing to you his call to service, and for your affirming response. Confess your deafness, blindness, hardheartedness, and excuses that keep you from hearing and responding to God's call (3:6, 11, 13). Commit yourself to being aware of God's presence every day and listening to his call to service, no matter how humbling that service may be. Ask him to give you a positive attitude in carrying out his call.

For Your Family and Friends

Pray that your family and friends will hold you accountable to fulfill God's calling for you.

For the Church

Pray that God will call forth leadership from your church who will "be careful" how they live, "not as unwise, but as wise" (Eph. 5:15).

For the Kingdom

Pray that you be hospitable, loving what is good, self-controlled, upright, holy and disciplined, holding firmly to the truth (Titus 1:8), thus growing God's kingdom on the inside.

For the Unsaved

Pray that God will use you to encourage others by sound teaching and the ability to refute those who oppose it (1:9), and so open doors of salvation to those for whom God has prepared it.

JULY 25

Personal Prayer

Praise God for his non-condemning attitude (Jn. 8:10-11), which gives you hope when you fail. Give thanks for help in seeing the "plank" in your own eyes before looking at the "specks" in another's (Mt. 7:3). Confess the many times you judge by appearance rather than by facts (Jn. 7:24). Commit yourself to God's judgment (1 Cor. 11:32), and be disciplined by him, learning from your mistakes (Heb. 12:10-11). Ask God to help you learn from other's judgments of you.

For Your Family and Friends

Pray for God's help to be generous in affirming your family and friends, rather than misjudging them or their motives (Ps. 119:66).

For the Church

Pray that your church will warmly welcome anyone, regardless of race, color, financial resources, etc., and take the lead in having all guests feel welcome (Heb. 13:1-2).

For the Kingdom

Pray that sound judgment and discernment will be preserved throughout God's kingdom (Prov. 3:21), resulting in kingdom growth.

For the Unsaved

Pray that your loving and nonjudgmental attitude toward one who has wronged you will give you opportunity to present Christ to that person, realizing God will bring every deed into judgment (Eccl. 12:14).

JULY 26

Personal Prayer

Praise God for the example of servanthood given when Jesus washed the disciples' feet (Jn. 13:5-15). Thank Jesus for his promise that you will be blessed in being a servant, following his example (13:17). Confess those times you are quarrelsome and resentful, not wanting to be a servant (2 Tim. 2:24). Commit yourself to God as Samuel did and respond: "Speak, for your servant is listening" (1 Sam. 3:10). Ask God to reveal clearly his assigned task for you, even as he did for Paul (1 Cor. 3:5).

For Your Family and Friends

Pray that by faithfully obeying God's commands to be servants, your family members will see God's blessing in their lives and praise him always (Deut. 11:13-15).

For the Church

Pray that your church will faithfully learn the joy of servanthood in every area, fixing their eyes on Jesus, not growing weary or losing heart (Heb. 12:2-3).

For the Kingdom

Pray that Christians everywhere will "serve faithfully and wholeheartedly in the fear of the LORD" (2 Chron. 19:9).

For the Unsaved

Pray for an opportunity to be a witness today as a loving servant to an unsaved friend or neighbor (Gal. 5:13).

Prayer Pointer

"Simply to say prayers is not to pray; otherwise a team of properly trained parrots would serve as well as men in prayer."—C. S. LEWIS

JULY 27

Personal Prayer

Praise God, who teaches you to pray "not as I will, but as you will" (Mt. 26:39). Thank God for his counsel as you set the Lord always before you, thus keeping you from being shaken in any circumstance (Ps. 16:7-8). Confess your struggle with God's will when you are tempted to fail him as you see the world prospering (Ps. 73:1-22). Commit yourself to God anew today, knowing he holds you with his right hand, guides and counsels you, and will take you to glory (73:23-28). Ask the Lord for the assurance that whenever you come to him, he will never drive you away (Jn. 6:37).

For Your Family and Friends

Pray that you may see how God often works out his will for you by using family and friends. Give thanks for that (Es. 4:13-14).

For the Church

Pray that your church will challenge everyone who attends to seek God's will and counsel, resulting in a renewed interest in community outreach ministries as well as in world missions.

For the Kingdom

Pray that God's kingdom will be advanced by your willingness to do whatever God may require of you and to do it joyfully (Acts 21:13-14).

For the Unsaved

Pray that whenever you open your mouth, words will be given you so that you may fearlessly make known the gospel whenever the opportunity presents itself (Eph. 6:19).

JULY 28

Personal Prayer

Praise God for his compelling love (2 Cor. 5:14). Give thanks for that love that holds us as in a vice, never letting go (Jer. 31:3). Confess those times when you fight against God's love, wanting to go your own way or seek glory for yourself instead of for him. Commit yourself to being comfortable in that "love grip" of God so that you willingly live for him, serving him gladly (Prov. 3:3-6). Ask God to give you a greater appreciation of his eternal blessings and to be glad with the joy of his presence (Ps. 21:6).

For Your Family and Friends

Pray that your family and friends will not be threatened by God's compelling love but will rest secure in him as he shields them (Deut. 33:12).

For the Church

Pray that God's unfailing love will satisfy every member of the church so that all may "sing for joy and be glad all our days" (Ps. 90:14).

For the Kingdom

Pray that God's compelling love may keep believers from fear and lead them on in the daily work of ministry "in Jerusalem, and Judea . . . and to the ends of the earth" (Joel 2:21-27; Acts 1:8).

For the Unsaved

Pray that this love will give you boldness in being a witness of your joy in the Lord by word and in deed to many this week.

JULY 29

Personal Prayer

Praise God that birth and conception are miraculous and a special gift from God. Thank him for planning all your days before you were even born (Ps. 139:16). Confess any dissatisfaction over the gifts and abilities God has given you. Commit yourself to God daily and, like Paul, be content in whatever situation he has placed you (Phil. 4:11). Ask God to bring personal peace as a member of your family.

For Your Family and Friends

Pray that children in your family circle and among your friends may be blessed with godly parents who are good examples and who discipline them in love (Prov. 22:6).

For the Church

Pray that children's ministries may have an important role in your church and that children will happily invite their friends to participate in these activities with them.

For the Kingdom

Praise God for the children of missionaries, that they may share the love of Jesus among their friends.

For the Unsaved

Pray that unsaved children who attend Bible classes with friends will bring that gospel message to their own homes as well (Mt. 11:25).

Prayer Pointer

"Work as if everything depended upon work and pray as if everything depended upon prayer." —William Booth

JULY 30

Personal Prayer

Praise "God, the Father Almighty, Creator of heaven and earth." Thank him for being your Father through Christ Jesus. Confess tendencies to act like a spiritual orphan. Commit yourself to more consistently remembering the responsibilities and privileges of being God's child. Ask him to help you bring honor to the family name.

For Your Family and Friends

Pray that all your friends and members of your family will truly be part of God's family. Ask God to help each one look beyond imperfect human parents to God as the perfect Father.

For the Church

Pray that your local congregation will bring pleasure to the Father through its weekly worship times. Ask God to help all members and regular attendees act with true family love toward one another.

For the Kingdom

Pray that the diverse groups of Christian believers will recognize that all are in the same family. Ask the Father to help believers to get along with brothers and sisters.

For the Unsaved

Pray that people throughout the world will acknowledge their Creator as their Father through Jesus Christ.

JULY 31

Personal Prayer

Praise "Jesus Christ, his only Son, our Lord." Thank him for his willingness to leave his heavenly home to live among sinners. Confess any way in which you have been unwilling to sacrifice in order to come alongside those in need. Commit yourself to having the attitude of Jesus (Phil. 2:5-11). Ask God to give you that selfless love.

For Your Family and Friends

Pray that you will consistently bring the presence of Jesus to those with whom you live. Ask Jesus to help you focus more on loving than on being loved.

For the Church

Pray that your local church will be known as a group where one can readily sense the presence, as well as the truths, of Jesus Christ. Ask Jesus to especially shine through your church's leaders.

For the Kingdom

Pray that the presence of Christ in his people will be a "salting" and "lighting" influence throughout the earth. Ask God to maintain full integrity in national and international media ministries.

For the Unsaved

Pray that the presence of Jesus through you will effectively draw an unsaved neighbor to him. Ask God to give you the right actions, words, and love in your community.

Prayer Pointer

"It is in recognizing the actual presence of God that we find prayer no longer a chore, but a supreme delight." —Gordon Lindsay

AUGUST 1

Personal Prayer

Praise God for his power to do the miraculous. Give thanks for the miracle of Jesus being "conceived by the Holy Spirit and born of the virgin Mary." Confess any difficulties in believing that he has done what the Scriptures say he has done. Commit to believing in God's ability to do the miraculous in your life. Ask God to give you a bigger view of himself.

For Your Family and Friends

Pray that the mystery of God's power will produce awe in a family member or friend who seems a bit flippant about God. Ask God to lift up Jesus through you.

For the Church

Pray that Christ will be lifted up in your local church, drawing all people to himself. Ask God to call true believers away from any false religious practices and out of false churches.

For the Kingdom

Pray that Christ's people around the world will be faithful to move as his force into their communities. Ask God to move with supernatural power to bring whole groups to the divine Savior.

For the Unsaved

Pray that God will supernaturally increase the effectiveness of the outreach ministries of your local church. Ask him to use you in that great effort.

AUGUST 2

Personal Prayer

Praise Jesus as the suffering servant. Thank him for the love that brought him to the point where he "suffered under Pontius Pilate, was crucified, died, and was buried" and even "descended to hell" for you. Confess any lack of appreciation for such love. Commit yourself to never misusing the name of such a loving Savior. Ask him to guide you in giving your life in thankful response.

For Your Family and Friends

Pray that all of your close contacts will come to a deeper understanding of how much their sin cost Jesus. Ask God to save each one.

For the Church

Pray for those in the education ministries of your local church and broader church assemblies. Ask God to generate awe and love for Jesus through their teaching about his sacrifice.

For the Kingdom

Pray for the Christians whom God has called to be teachers throughout the week. Ask God to motivate them with the giving love of Jesus.

For the Unsaved

Pray that unsaved students will be drawn to the Savior through their teachers. Ask God to show them their unmistakable need for the one who was crucified to bring them real knowledge and real life.

Prayer Pointer

"Because God is the living God, he can hear; because he is a loving God, he will hear; because he is our covenant God, he has bound himself to hear."
—Charles H. Spurgeon

AUGUST 3

Personal Prayer

Praise Jesus as the one who "rose again from the dead" and "ascended to heaven" where he is "seated at the right hand of God the Father almighty." Thank God for access to him through Jesus the Intercessor. Confess any skepticism of God's willingness to hear your prayers. Commit yourself to living under the flag of King Jesus today. Ask the ascended King to rule over even the details of your life.

For Your Family and Friends

Pray that the children in your circle of close contacts will know that they belong to the King of heaven and earth. Ask God to help you model the dignity of living for Jesus.

For the Church

Pray for world missionaries who are calling groups of people to bow before Jesus. Ask that these groups' rulers and leaders also submit and begin to lead their people in Jesus' ways.

For the Kingdom

Pray for "all those in authority, that we may live peaceful and quiet lives in all godliness and holiness" (1 Tim. 2:2). Ask that the peaceful rule of Jesus might soon come in fullness.

For the Unsaved

Pray that unsaved acquaintances will submit to Jesus before he comes "to judge the living and the dead." Ask God to give you a sense of the urgency of bringing the good news to them.

AUGUST 4

Personal Prayer

As one who professes to "believe in the Holy Spirit," praise God for his indwelling of all believers. Give thanks for his intimacy and power. Confess any tendency to rely on your own strength rather than God's. Commit to becoming more sensitive to God's ongoing presence. Ask God to increase your consciousness of continual companionship with him.

For Your Family and Friends

Pray that the Holy Spirit will fill each of your family and friends, bringing a deep sense of his presence. Ask him to fill your household with his power.

For the Church

Pray that we who have been richly blessed by the "fellowship with the Spirit" might be "like-minded, having the same love, being one in spirit and purpose" (Phil. 2:1-2). Ask God to move with power through any such spirituality.

For the Kingdom

Pray for God to move with his Spirit to bring true revival to your country. Ask God to move powerfully at your place of work.

For the Unsaved

Pray that the oneness of God's people will draw the unsaved to him. Ask the Spirit to convict unsaved acquaintances of their sin and convince them to turn in faith to God.

Prayer Pointer

"Prayers not felt by us are seldom heard by God."—Philip Henry

AUGUST 5

Personal Prayer

Praise God as the Creator, Father, Savior, Lord, and indwelling Spirit of his church. Give thanks for "the holy catholic church, the communion of saints; the forgiveness of sins; the resurrection of the body, and the life everlasting." Reflecting with God on how you aid or damage his church, confess any sin he reveals. Commit to being a helpful member of God's community. Ask him to work through you to serve and enrich others.

For Your Family and Friends

Pray for each member of your household to forget what is behind and strain toward what is ahead, pressing on toward the goal to win the prize for which God has called them heavenward in Christ Jesus (Phil. 3:13-14).

For the Church

Pray for each member of Christ's body to excellently manage the treasures and gifts placed in his or her care. Ask God to prompt you to loving and generous service.

For the Kingdom

Pray for financial needs to be abundantly met in various efforts to advance God's kingdom around the world. Ask God for vision as well as finances.

For the Unsaved

Ask God to draw people to himself through your generous love.

AUGUST 6

Personal Prayer

Read Ps. 47:5-8 and praise with joy your God, who has ascended amid the sound of trumpets. Thank him for being the King of all the earth, for reigning over the nations. Confess that you often do not think of God in such lofty terms. Commit yourself to praising God wholeheartedly today. Ask God to reveal himself to you as you praise him.

For Your Family and Friends

Does your family sing together in praise of God? Try it today! And pray that God will give each member of your family a joyful heart in praising God.

For the Church

"God is seated on his holy throne" (47:8). Pray that your congregation will have a true sense of God's holiness and majesty as they worship week by week. Pray that every part of your worship will be directed to this God.

For the Kingdom

Ask God to be in the midst of his people in every time zone as they bring a worldwide symphony of praise. Pray for an anointing of the Holy Spirit in every place of worship.

For the Unsaved

Ask God to touch the lives of unsaved people today. Pray that some will hear the gospel and fall in repentance and faith at the foot of the cross.

AUGUST 7

Personal Prayer

Read Ps. 40:1-3 and praise your Redeemer and Savior. Thank God for lifting you up out of the mud and mire of sin. Confess those times you've desired to return to the slimy pit of sin. Commit yourself to living in such a way that others may "see . . . and put their trust in the LORD." Ask God to enable you to stand firm on the Rock of Jesus Christ.

For Your Family and Friends

Pray that Jesus the Rock will be the foundation and cornerstone of your family. Ask especially that teens you know will find a firm place to stand in Christ.

For the Church

Today pray especially for the leaders of your congregation. Ask God to put a new song in the mouths of your elders, deacons, and pastor(s), that they will show forth his glory in the church.

For the Kingdom

Pray for the Church in communist countries. Thank God for the many thousands of believers who remain faithful despite oppression. Pray that the strongholds of Satan will be demolished in those lands.

For the Unsaved

Ask God to draw an unsaved friend to himself. Pray that God will equip you to share the gospel with that person in an appropriate way. Seek opportunities this week.

AUGUST 8

Personal Prayer

Read Ps. 73:23-26 and give praise to the one who holds you every day by your right hand. Thank God for guiding you by his wise counsel. Confess any time you have desired some earthly trinket more than the riches of your heavenly Father. Commit yourself to staying close to God today. Ask God to be "the strength of [your] heart and [your] portion forever."

For Your Family and Friends

Pray for any family members or friends who are straying away from God, who are trying desperately to pull free from God's loving handhold. Ask that they will turn back to God.

For the Church

Pray today for the outreach ministries of your congregation or denomination. Pray for those who lead these ministries. Ask that God will provide the funding necessary to reach out to those with spiritual and physical needs.

For the Kingdom

Ask for God's grace to fill those who minister comfort in the name of Christ to persons with AIDS. Pray that many who have contracted AIDS will find safety in the arms of Jesus.

For the Unsaved

Pray for any unsaved friends or relatives by name. Ask that they will embrace the peace that comes with having God hold them by the hand.

AUGUST 9

Personal Prayer

Read Ps. 86:15-17 and praise God for his marvelous compassion, grace, love, and faithfulness to you. Thank him for turning to you and having mercy on you. Confess any lack of appreciation for God's saving work in your life. Commit yourself to loving God wholeheartedly in response to his love for you. Ask God to give you a sign of his goodness.

For Your Family and Friends

Pray for God's mercy to be shown to any family member or friend in need. Ask the Lord to provide abundantly from his storehouses of grace.

For the Church

Ask God's blessing on the educational programs of your church. Pray for each teacher and helper. Ask God to show you how you might be involved in the instruction of others.

For the Kingdom

Pray that the enemies of God will be put to shame throughout his kingdom. Ask that the forces of the evil one will be destroyed and that justice, righteousness, and peace might prevail on the earth.

For the Unsaved

Ask that people in your neighborhood who do not yet know Jesus will be drawn to him by observing your Christlike behavior. Pray that they will have the boldness to ask about the faith they see in you.

Prayer Pointer

"God has chosen prayer as the key by which his church does its work. Through prayer we impact the world for God." —Anonymous

AUGUST 10

Personal Prayer

Read Ps. 91:1-2 and praise the Most High, the Almighty, the Lord, your God. Thank him for providing shelter and shade from the heat of spiritual conflict in your life. Confess those times when you've sought shelter other than that provided by the Most High. Commit yourself to simply resting in God. Ask him always to be your refuge and fortress in every life situation.

For Your Family and Friends

Pray that your home will be a resting place, a shelter where you and your family can find peace, quiet, and safety. Ask that your children will sense the security of a home built on the love of Jesus.

For the Church

Pray for the work of missionaries throughout the world who carry the gospel in word and deed into sometimes hostile countries. Pray especially for those working in Muslim countries. Ask that they will be sheltered by the Most High.

For the Kingdom

Pray for those who take the liberating love of Christ into prisons throughout the world. Ask God to bless those prisoners who have trusted Christ, but must remain behind bars. Pray for their safety and testimony to other prisoners.

For the Unsaved

Ask God to be a refuge and fortress to many unsaved who are being blown about the wild winds of secularism. Pray that they will find shelter in Christ.

AUGUST 11

Personal Prayer

Read Ps. 139:13-17 and praise the God who knit you together in your mother's womb. Give thanks for all of his wonderful works. Confess those moments when foolishly you've tried to hide from God. Commit yourself to living each day with the full assurance that God has written each one in his book. Ask that today you might be reminded of God's precious thoughts toward you.

For Your Family and Friends

Today thank God for your children or grandchildren. Think of how marvelously complex their bodies are. Pray for any of them who suffer from physical or mental impairments.

For the Church

Pray that caregiving and fellowship in your congregation will grow. Ask God to open the eyes of your church members to needs which they can meet.

For the Kingdom

Pray for those organizations throughout North America which promote the sanctity of human life. Ask God to put down the evil of abortion on demand. Pray that parents in your city or community who are considering abortion today will choose an alternative to preserve the life of their unborn child.

For the Unsaved

Pray for an unsaved friend by name. Ask God to enter into that person's conscience. Pray that he or she will become aware of God's plan of salvation through Jesus Christ. Ask God to make you ready to answer your friend's questions.

AUGUST 12

Personal Prayer

Read Ps. 148:7-14 and "let yourself go" as you praise God with all of creation. Thank God for his wonderful works, which join in praise to the Creator. Confess any times you have failed to value the creation or have misused it in any way. Commit yourself to maintaining an attitude of praise to God throughout this day. Ask that God's name will be praised throughout all the earth.

For Your Family and Friends

If you are married, intercede for your spouse. Pray for his or her walk with the Lord. Pray for marriages among your friends, asking that they will be grounded in Christ's love.

For the Church

Pray for the financial stewardship of your congregation. Pray that the members will have great joy in giving to the work of the Lord. Ask God's blessing on the deacons of your church as they manage financial resources.

For the Kingdom

Pray for all the schools of your community. Intercede for Christian teachers, school board members, and administrators in public schools. Ask God to prosper the work of Christian schools and colleges as well.

For the Unsaved

Pray that unsaved individuals you know will soon join "the people close to [God's] heart" (148:14) and the creation in praising the majestic name of the Lord.

AUGUST 13

Personal Prayer

Praise Jesus, who is "declared with power to be the Son of God by his resurrection from the dead" (Rom. 1:4). Thank the Father for having given us his "incomparably great power . . . the working of his mighty strength, which he exerted in Christ when he raised him from the dead" (Eph. 1:19-20). Confess the times when you have not taken into account the mighty power of God in your life. Commit yourself to meditating daily on the Scriptures and on the power of God (Mt. 22:29). Ask God to use your weaknesses to "show that this all-surpassing power is from God and not from us" (2 Cor. 4:7).

For Your Family and Friends

Ask God that your own reliance on his strength will be an encouragement and inspiration to family and friends who struggle with sin and weakness.

For the Church

Pray that those worshiping this Sunday may sense God's power moving in the worship service—to cleanse, to heal, to change lives.

For the Kingdom

Ask God to raise up preachers and teachers who will fearlessly proclaim his Word with power in all countries of the world.

For the Unsaved

Pray for God's power to be unleashed in the life of the unsaved people you know, that their eyes will be opened to God's love for them.

AUGUST 14

Personal Prayer

Praise God as the Father of the fatherless and the defender of the helpless. Give thanks that, even in large cities, God's eye is on the small and defenseless and alone (Jon. 4:11). Confess those times when you have not remembered by prayer or material aid those in your community who have needed your help (Mt. 25:35-40). Commit yourself to looking at others through the compassionate eyes of your Father. Ask him to pull you out of your comfort zone and into the needs of others.

For Your Family and Friends

Ask God to help you see where other family members feel helpless or alone and to allow you to bear their burdens with them (Gal. 6:2).

For the Church

Pray for your leaders, that they will model God's compassion in reaching out to the lonely and the helpless in your community.

For the Kingdom

Ask God to bless, financially and spiritually, his churches' programs in your area for the poor and homeless.

For the Unsaved

Pray that unsaved people in your community will be so moved by your church's compassion toward strangers and outsiders that they will be drawn into God's family.

Prayer Pointer

"No one is a firmer believer in the power of prayer than the devil; not that he practices it, but he suffers from it." —Guy H. King

AUGUST 15

Personal Prayer

Praise God for his heart that is open, warm, loving, and kind toward all he has made. Thank God for reaching down to draw you to himself through his Son (Jn. 3:16). Confess the times when your heart has been unwilling to give to others the same out-reaching love that you have received from God. Commit yourself to learning the kind, patient love of God (1 Cor. 13:4). Ask him to fill you with a knowledge of the depth and breadth of his love (Eph. 3:14-19).

For Your Family and Friends

Pray for those marriages or parent/child relationships where love is lacking and where the home is a battleground. Ask God to heal their brokenness with his love.

For the Church

Ask God to make his love the hallmark of your church's outreach programs, so that neighbors will sense the genuine interest and care of the family of God.

For the Kingdom

Intercede for the specific caring ministries that your church or denomination is involved in worldwide, asking that broken lives and poverty-stricken families may be helped.

For the Unsaved

Ask God to show you what act of loving concern you can do this week for an unsaved friend or acquaintance.

AUGUST 16

Personal Prayer

Praise God, whose mind and imagination created the stars, the earth, and the life of all creatures. Give thanks for the reaches of God's knowledge, which far exceeds the limits of the human mind. Confess the times in this past week when you have leaned on your own understanding and not followed the teachings of the Lord (Hos. 14:9). Commit yourself to studying the Bible regularly to learn what God has to teach you. Ask the Lord to make his Word as sweet as honey (Ps. 19:10).

For Your Family and Friends

Pray for young adults and their parents, that the teaching of the Lord may be a living faith passed down from parent to child.

For the Church

Pray for each of your church education teachers, that they may be powerful examples by their words and behavior and may be aware of their great responsibility (Jas. 3:1).

For the Kingdom

Pray for the writers and editors of your church's education materials and those who train others to use them, that they may present God's teachings in a fresh way and inspire church education teachers to model their faith effectively in the classroom.

For the Unsaved

Pray that the Christian reading materials developed for adult beginning readers—the illiterate, refugees, immigrants, and others—may reach their hearts with the gospel.

AUGUST 17

Personal Prayer

From your heart give praise to God as the Father of all peoples, the one from whom every family on earth derives its name (Eph. 3:14-15). Thank him for having created such a wide variety of peoples and cultures, including your own. Confess those times when you have looked down on people simply because their culture or way of life is different from yours. Commit yourself to learning more about the people who live and work around you. Ask God to help you become genuinely interested in other people's perspectives as you pray for opportunities to share the good news with them.

For Your Family and Friends

Ask God to restore any breaches between the generations that you are aware of—frictions between grandparents and parents or grandchildren, and so on.

For the Church

Pray for your church's missionaries in war-torn countries, that they may remain safe and may present the light of hope and love in the midst of despair, hatred, and destruction.

For the Kingdom

Pray for the leaders of those countries, that they may acknowledge the lordship of Jesus Christ and his authority in their lives. Ask for justice and peace to be restored to their governments, along with an end to racial hatreds or prejudices.

For the Unsaved

Pray for the new immigrants to North America, that they may hear the gospel and be drawn into the church's fellowship.

AUGUST 18

Personal Prayer

Praise the one who is before all things, the one in whom all things hold together, the head of the church (Col. 1:17-18). Thank Christ for making peace between you and God by his blood shed on the cross. Confess those times when you have allowed something to come between you and another believer, weakening your unity in Christ. Commit yourself to seeking better understanding of that person's position and feelings. Ask God to help you see the unity that exists between all followers of Christ.

For Your Friends and Family

Pray for those families who have shut out unbelieving members. Ask for God's outreaching love to bring them back into the family circle.

For the Church

Ask God to reconcile differences in your congregation over worship style, outreach, and so on. Pray for a spirit of unity and humility (Phil. 2:1-4).

For the Kingdom

Pray that differences between denominations worldwide will not keep believers from praying and worshiping together and from working side by side in missions.

For the Unsaved

Pray for unbelievers in the media. Ask that God may allow them to see such unity in the church that they will have to acknowledge the reality of Jesus Christ (Jn. 17:23).

Prayer Pointer

"Make prayer the time to give yourself this day as a gift to God." —The Praying Church Sourcebook

AUGUST 19

Personal Prayer

Give praise to Jesus as the manna that has come down from heaven, the bread of life who nourishes the hungry with himself (Jn. 6:48-51). Thank him for taking care of your spiritual as well as your physical needs. Confess those times during the past week when you have failed to come to Jesus in prayer in order to receive all that you need. Commit yourself to spending more time in his presence. Ask Jesus to show you his power to take care of all the desires of your heart (Mt. 6:33).

For Your Family and Friends

Ask God to give parents wisdom in teaching their children how to give a part of their income, no matter how small, to God. Pray that through this giving, children may learn to trust in their heavenly Father's ability to provide.

For the Church

Lay before God the financial needs of your congregation and ask God to show those who work with finances the best way to use the monies that have been offered.

For the Kingdom

Pray for generous giving to meet the desperate needs of those stricken with famine, earthquake, war, floods, or other disasters. Ask God to use such giving as a powerful witness to the gospel (2 Cor. 9:10-14).

For the Unsaved

Pray for the unsaved people you know who struggle with a shortage of money. Ask God to use these circumstances to turn them to him for help, through the generosity of the church.

AUGUST 20

Personal Prayer

Praise God that he promises to refresh you like the dew from heaven in order to blossom as the lily (Hos. 14:5). Give thanks for the beauty of flowers, a beauty to be reflected in the life of every Christian. Confess to God the times you disguise that beauty with outward circumstances which keep you from reflecting his image (Col. 3:5-10). Commit yourself to being clothed with compassion, kindness, humility, gentleness, patience, and especially love, which binds believers together in unity (3:12-14). Ask God to root out the weeds and let the beauty of Jesus be seen in you.

For Your Family and Friends

Pray that your family and friends may see the real inward beauty of your life reflecting Jesus, which makes your outward appearance beautiful at all times (1 Sam. 16:7).

For the Church

Ask that the beauty of your worship experiences will glorify God alone.

For the Kingdom

Pray that all teachers and preachers who handle the Word of God will preach and teach in God's strength, not with words of human wisdom, lest the cross of Christ be emptied of its power (1 Cor. 1:17).

For the Unsaved

Ask that you will not use flattery in your witness to unsaved friends, but rather honestly encourage and comfort them, urging them to be open to Christ (1 Thess. 2:4, 11-13).

AUGUST 21

Personal Prayer

Praise God for his teaching on the tongue (Jas. 3:9). Give thanks that he promises protection from the lash of the tongue (Job 5:21) and healing from the tongue of the wise (Prov. 12:18). Confess those times your lips have spoken lies and your tongue muttered wicked things (Isa. 59:3). Commit yourself to God, who gives you the words that will sustain the weary (Isa. 50:4). Ask God to help you love not just with words or tongue but with actions and in truth (1 Jn. 3:18).

For Your Family and Friends

Pray that God will help you to be honest in all you do and say to your family and friends because "a lying tongue hates those it hurts and a flattering mouth works ruin" (Prov. 26:28).

For the Church

Ask that your church leaders will be good examples in their speech and conduct especially since "the mouth of the righteous man utters wisdom, and his tongue speaks what is just" (Ps. 37:30).

For the Kingdom

Pray that fear of speaking will not hold back Christians from being a witness. Ask that God will assure them as he did Moses, that he will help them speak (Ex. 4:10-12).

For the Unsaved

Pray that the testimony of your lips overflowing in praise and your tongue singing God's Word will be evident to non-Christians and point them to Christ (Ps. 119:171-172).

AUGUST 22

Personal Prayer

Praise God that even though you were once an enemy of God, he has reconciled you by Christ's physical body through death (Col. 1:21-22). Give thanks that you are now alive with Christ, without blemish and free from accusation (Col. 2:13). Confess your failure to live up to that holiness, praying, "God, have mercy on me, a sinner" (Lk. 18:13). Commit yourself to rejoicing when you are called to share in the suffering of Christ (1 Pet. 4:13-14). Ask God to help you see the victory you are given in Jesus as you trust the Holy Spirit to guide you in being his image-bearer (1 Cor. 15:57).

For Your Family and Friends

Some of your family may not sense victory in Jesus because of physical pain. Pray that the grace of Jesus will be sufficient for them (2 Cor. 12:9).

For the Church

All churches experience the pain of divorce, broken homes, and death. Pray that those who have overcome such difficult experiences as these may effectively reach out to others in similar situations.

For the Kingdom

Claim God's promise to defend the afflicted and to crush the oppressor (Ps. 72:4).

For the Unsaved

Pray for God to use some painful experience in your life as a means to reach an unbeliever with salvation (2 Cor. 1:3-7).

AUGUST 23

Personal Prayer

Praise God for his unconditional love (1 Corinthians 13). Thank him for showing you in Christ how to love others unconditionally. Confess your lack of love when you've failed to meet God's standards and requirements. Commit yourself to allowing his love to flow naturally through you, resulting in spontaneous acts of love (1 Jn. 3:18). Ask God to let the Holy Spirit work in you daily so that "love deeds" are a "natural" way of life.

For Your Family and Friends

Pray that God will use his love in you as a magnet to draw your family and friends closer to him and to each other.

For the Church

Pray that all your church staff may be rooted and established in love and have the power and ability to communicate God's love to all with whom they have contact (Eph. 3:17-19).

For the Kingdom

Ask that all kingdom workers serve together in love (Gal. 5:13) and communicate the important message that what really counts in life is faith expressing itself in love (5:6).

For the Unsaved

Pray that God will help you do something spontaneous today to reflect his love to one who is outside of the family of God (Lk. 6:27-31).

Prayer Pointer

"True prayer is a way of life, not just a case of emergency." —Anonymous

AUGUST 24

Personal Prayer

Praise God that he is your stronghold in time of trouble (Ps. 9:9). Give thanks for God's promise that when you call on him in the day of trouble, he will deliver you (Ps. 50:15). Confess your failure to glorify and honor God when he does give you deliverance. Commit yourself to keeping the vows you make when you are in trouble (Ps. 66:13-16). Ask God to bring you to your knees in every situation, not just when special trouble surrounds you (Psalm 116).

For Your Family and Friends

Ask God to use your testimony of his faithfulness in time of trouble to help your family grow in God's love and see his purpose for their lives.

For the Church

Praise God for your church's efforts in supporting world missions. Pray that missionaries who must raise their own support will be rewarded for their trust in God to supply all their needs.

For the Kingdom

Pray that all Christians will see God's hand in trouble and trials knowing that "God . . . will pay back trouble to those who trouble you" (2 Thess. 1:6).

For the Unsaved

Pray that God will use a victory you've experienced to be a means of salvation for an unsaved friend this week.

AUGUST 25

Personal Prayer

Praise God that he sweeps away your offenses like the morning mist (Isa. 44:22). Give thanks that God is not unjust and will not forget your work and the love you have shown him as you help others (Heb. 6:10). Confess to him those secret things you do which you know are wrong but just haven't been able to confess (Ps. 44:21). Commit yourself to building others up with encouragement and ridding yourself of bitterness and anger, forgiving others as God in Christ forgives you (Eph. 4:29-32). Ask God to help you be an imitator of him, living a life of love (Eph. 5:1).

For Your Family and Friends

Pray that God will give you his strength to "right some wrong" that you have committed against a family member or friend.

For the Church

Pray that your church will be a forgiving, loving church that is open to receiving any who come, without judging them in any way (Mt. 7:1).

For the Kingdom

Pray for God's kingdom to grow in his people with a concern to love Jesus more and more, to read the Word faithfully, and not try to build self by judging others.

For the Unsaved

Ask that a positive act of forgiveness on your part will lead an unbelieving friend to attend church with you this week and seek faith in Christ.

AUGUST 26

Personal Prayer

Praise God that "though he brings grief, he will show compassion . . . for he does not willingly bring affliction or grief to the children of men" (Lam. 3:32-33). Give thanks for God's promise that your grief will be turned to joy (Jn. 16:20). Confess to him the times you let grief or affliction turn to bitterness or unconfessed sin. Commit yourself to allowing these trials or afflictions to be a stepping stone to a greater faith. Ask God to help you guard yourself in your spirit and do not break faith (Mal. 2:16).

For Your Family and Friends

Pray that your family will see that affliction can be good (Ps. 119:71), that in faithfulness God may afflict, and that his unfailing love will be their comfort (119:75-76).

For the Church

Ask that financial pressure in your congregation will draw you together in prayer and trust, and move you forward in faith as you share with those in need (Rom. 12:12-13).

For the Kingdom

Pray that God will continue to build his kingdom in areas of the world where there is oppression, hunger, and lack of resources.

For the Unsaved

Ask that God will use you today to give comfort to the afflicted who do not know Christ, assuring them that your God will supply all their needs (Phil. 4:19).

AUGUST 27

Personal Prayer

Praise "God, from whom all blessings flow!" Thank him for making his blessings available to you in Christ Jesus. Confess that you are spiritually poor in yourself. Commit yourself to gratitude to God for replacing your poverty with all the treasures of "the kingdom of heaven" (Mt. 5:3). Ask for a renewed appreciation for this tremendous, gracious exchange.

For Your Family and Friends

Thank God for family members and friends who also have experienced God's exchange of their poverty for his riches.

For the Church

Pray that those worshiping God this week will come acknowledging, "Nothing in my hand I bring . . . helpless, look to Thee for grace." Ask for a profound sense of gratitude in your congregation's worship.

For the Kingdom

Pray that Christian believers throughout the world will truly celebrate what God does in Christ.

For the Unsaved

Pray for those caught in addictions to drugs, sex, self-reliance, etc., to admit that they are powerless to overcome these evils by themselves. Ask God to use you this week to point at least one person to him and his resources.

Prayer Pointer

"Prayer becomes a battleground where we wrestle with what it means to live God's life in the world."—Maxie Dunnam

AUGUST 28

Personal Prayer

Praise God, "the Father of compassion and the God of all comfort" (2 Cor. 1:3). Give thanks for God's comfort to you and all who truly mourn (Mt. 5:4). Confess any sin he shows you, truly mourning for the pain you have caused. Commit to receiving God's forgiveness. Ask the Lord to search your heart and thoughts, removing any offensive way and leading you "in the way everlasting" (Ps. 139:23-24).

For Your Family and Friends

Pray for those close to you to know God's comforting forgiveness. Ask God to effectively bring that to them through you.

For the Church

Pray that the leaders of your congregation and denomination will be persons who truthfully confront sin in themselves and in those they lead. Ask that they be clear channels of God's forgiving comfort.

For the Kingdom

Pray that the righteousness of Christ will be evidenced to your whole community through your church's leadership and membership. Ask God to help you keep his kingdom and righteousness your first priority.

For the Unsaved

Pray that the unsaved will not merely complain in the misery caused by their sins nor seek acceptance of their sins. Ask that they will be moved by God's Spirit to truly mourn in the sorrow of repentance and thereby be open to his healing and comfort.

AUGUST 29

Personal Prayer

Praise the Lord as the one who owns the earth and everything in it (Ps. 24:1). Thank him for making it part of the inheritance of the meek (Mt. 5:5). Confess aspects of your life where you do not have the meekness of submission to Christ's Lordship. Commit yourself to being filled and controlled by Christ. Ask him to properly bring the areas you influence under his influence.

For Your Family and Friends

Pray for any in your circle who are "out of control" or merely under the control of themselves. Ask God to reign in your home.

For the Church

Pray for outreach ministries, including various well-known evangelists, to be in proper accountability with God's people. Ask that the meekness of their submission to Christ's lordship far surpass their human appeal.

For the Kingdom

Pray that Christians in leadership positions in all walks of life be submitted to Christ. Ask that their meekness will allow those they influence to see past the human leaders to Christ.

For the Unsaved

Pray that the meekness of Christian leaders will pave the way for unsaved people to come to Christ.

AUGUST 30

Personal Prayer

Praise Jesus as the righteous one. Thank God that "you are in Christ Jesus, who has become for us wisdom from God—that is, our righteousness, holiness and redemption" (1 Cor. 1:30). Confess any desire to dabble in unrighteousness in any corner of your life. Commit yourself to hungering and thirsting for righteousness, asking God to fill you (Mt. 5:6).

For Your Family and Friends

Pray for your family and friends to turn away from godless and evil television programs, videos, music, and magazines.

For the Church

Pray for church education personnel to excellently teach God's truth and model its application. Ask that right thinking with right living will be the trademark of your congregation's members.

For the Kingdom

Pray that the righteousness of Christ will shine through you so clearly and consistently that those around you "see your good deeds and praise your Father in heaven" (5:16).

For the Unsaved

Thank God for the gospel, the power of God for the salvation of everyone who believes (Rom. 1:16). Ask that a great hunger and thirst for Christ will be created in an unsaved person in your neighborhood.

AUGUST 31

Personal Prayer

Praise "God, who is rich in mercy" (Eph. 2:4). Give thanks that, in that great mercy, God has made you alive with Christ even when you were dead in transgressions (2:5). Confess situations where you've been unwilling to let God's mercy flow through you to someone who has wronged you. Commit to being merciful, knowing that this is where you also are shown mercy (Mt. 5:7). Ask God for the love and strength to be a merciful person.

For Your Family and Friends

Pray that your home will be a place dominated by compassion rather than severity. Ask God to cause his mercy to overflow from your home to your friends' homes.

For the Church

Pray for missionaries who are introducing people to the God who saves, not because of righteous human actions but because of his mercy (Titus 3:5). Ask God to make his mercy-bearing believers merciful to one another.

For the Kingdom

Pray for Christian relief workers and agencies showing compassion in the name of Christ. Ask for their safety in the midst of sometimes dangerous circumstances.

For the Unsaved

Pray that such forgiveness and compassion will prevail in the church that the world will know that Jesus has come with God's supernatural love (Jn. 17:23). Ask God to draw the unsaved to himself through that love.